Strolling with Your Elephant

PERFECT MOMENTS IN TRAVEL

For Jeffrey and Peter

ISBN: 979-8-9867378-1-2
Paperback ISBN: 979-8-9867378-0-5
Ebook ISBN: 979-8-9867378-2-9
Audio Book ISBN: 979-8-9867378-3-6

Design by Liliana Guia

Window Seat Press
New York

Strolling with Your Elephant

PERFECT MOMENTS IN TRAVEL

DIANA M. HECHLER

DESIGN BY LILIANA GUIA

Australia
8

Austria
18

Cambodia
26

Canada
30

Chile
40

Costa Rica
46

Croatia
50

Egypt
54

England
60

France
68

Germany
78

Iceland
86

Ireland
90

Italy
100

Japan
118

Jordan
126

Mexico
130

New Zealand
134

Peru
140

Scotland
148

Slovenia
154

South Africa
158

Spain
162

St. Maarten
172

Sweden
176

Switzerland
182

Thailand
188

Turkey
196

United States
200

Vietnam
212

Wales
220

FOREWORD

What is a perfect moment in travel? How do you make one happen? Where do you find it?

How much does it cost?

Perfect moments differ widely among us all. You may find that your stroll with an elephant brings you closer to the animal world than you ever dreamed possible. Your best friend might think that waltzing at a Viennese Ball in the historic Royal Palace makes her feel like Cinderella in the arms of her prince. Your significant other might discover his or her perfect moment climbing the Sydney Harbour Bridge and overlooking that magnificent harbor while standing in the sky.

Importantly, perfect moments carry price tags, from free to moderate to very expensive. It costs only the price of gasoline to trace John Wilkes Booth's path after his night at Ford's Theatre. On the other hand, chartering a rail car for twelve of your most intimate friends to coast the railroad tracks of Germany requires a deep pocket indeed.

The first time I ever defined a perfect moment for myself occurred on the island of Santorini. No, it wasn't a sunset cruise. I have taken the sunset cruise and it was fantastic, but my perfect moment was really quite simple.

I found myself on the island as part of a Greek Island cruise. I needed to run an errand involving a hotel with which I had done some business. Instead of setting off on a scheduled activity with other passengers, I took a taxi to the small town where the hotel is located. After I finished, I realized it was lunchtime. I chose a humble taverna with a view over the Aegean Sea. I sat down on the terrace. The waiter approached. I ordered a classic Greek Salad and a glass of the local white wine (retsina). The waiter brought me both, as well as some deliciously chewy bread. As I savored the simple but oh-so-fresh salad, I sipped my wine and stared out at the incredibly blue Aegean under the azure sky. The sea and sky melted into the distant horizon, and I couldn't tell where one ended and the other began. I sighed. I realized I was having a perfect moment during which I lacked for nothing. I was content. Eventually, I paid the minuscule bill and went on my way.

In my role as a travel advisor, I constantly strive to add "extras" to my clients' vacations. To that end, I always seek out special experiences to suggest they incorporate into their plans. I call this service, "You don't even know to ask me about it." Sometimes, the activity is a completely new concept. At other times, the traveler might have heard about the experience, but can't really understand what it is or that it's accessible to them. Climbing the Sydney Harbour Bridge is a good example.

On my first trip to Australia, I had seen the tiny little dots of people moving up over that tremendous arch. I had wondered, "Why would anyone want to do anything so foolhardy? It must be incredibly dangerous and scary." When I experienced Bridge Climb on a subsequent visit, I found that it was neither foolhardy nor particularly scary. (And I'm a bit of a chicken. I don't like roller coasters or horror movies.) By the time my group crested the arch, I was absolutely euphoric. See the chapter *Sydney Harbour Bridge Climb* for further details.

While making an "appointment" for a perfect moment is not really possible, you CAN put yourself in a position to make one occur. Whether you're exploring the back roads of Thailand, the Thermal Highway of New Zealand, the islands off Croatia, or the byways of rural Virginia, you can find your perfect moments everywhere. Let your own interests guide you.

Be aware that you can plan some of them yourself, but for others, you will need the services of a professional travel advisor with great connections worldwide.

Travel On!
Diana M. Hechler

AUSTRALIA

ALICE SPRINGS
OUTBACK
SYDNEY
ULURU (AYERS ROCK)

SCHOOL OF THE AIR

The Australian Outback is a vast desert of a place, comprising much of the center of this country/continent. All of the Northern Territory, most of Western Australia, South Australia, and Queensland, and the northwestern corner of New South Wales are part of the Outback. When you visit Uluru (Ayers Rock), you will glimpse the empty interior. Less than 5% of the nation's population lives there.

Yet some people DO live there. Small restaurants dot the major roads, providing services to travelers and locals. Ranchers and their families live on remote cattle stations. Rangers and their families stand watch over national parkland. Some of those families have children. How do they receive education, required by law for all residents age six to sixteen?

Your visit to The School of the Air in Alice Springs will illustrate how education is done in the Outback. Alice Springs, a small town in the remote interior of the Northern Territory, sits along the main road running from Adelaide in the south to Darwin on the northern coast. In 1872, a telegraph wire was strung along that road with booster stations at regular intervals. Alice Springs grew from a tiny booster station.

During World War I, a local minister decided to start a medical service to assist people living in the sparsely settled interior. With one plane and some distribution of radios, the Royal Flying Doctor Service was formed. Fast forward to 1944 when a school inspector visited Alice Springs and recognized that the existing correspondence courses made it difficult for the children of the Outback to learn effectively. Building on the idea of the radios used for the Royal Flying Doctor Service, she began to set up a radio-based system in which a live teacher would give a lesson three times a week by radio. The School of the Air was born.

At first, the school consisted of a one-way transmission, and the radios distributed were bicycle powered. In fact, one of the first things a young child would learn was how to operate the radio. Next came the means for a "Question and Answer" session after the lessons by a two-way transmission. Radios eventually gave way to televisions, and now the school and students use the internet.

You will find the School of the Air in a modest building. Teachers instruct their students in age-based classes from a modern studio with support offices nearby. Once a year, students come to Alice Springs with their families to meet their teacher and their classmates. In addition to special help for learning, the families and kids can socialize and enjoy normal peer-to-peer interaction.

After you tour this small facility, you will have an opportunity to donate a book to a student. There are plenty of books on hand to choose from, and there is a special insert for you to write a message to the recipient. Perhaps you will recognize and choose a favorite title from your own childhood. Or bring a copy with you and insert your note, telling the child what that book meant to you when you were growing up. Perhaps you will inscribe a message about living

on the opposite side of the world but seeing the same sun or moon or stars. It's your choice, but you can leave behind something tangible.

Since the Royal Flying Doctor Service is just a few blocks away, do stop in there, as well, to see the incredible network of medical services provided for the Outback residents. The live video feed of all the planes on their service calls will tell you everything you need to know.

KINGS CANYON RIM WALK

The empty Australia Outback takes up much of the center of this country/continent. Many first-time visitors to Australia fly to Ayers Rock to experience the local culture surrounding the sacred, gigantic outcropping known as Uluru (Ayers Rock). Perhaps they enjoy a side excursion to the other rock of Kata Tjuta as well.

If the season is right, pick up a rental car and head north toward Alice Springs. The drive through the stark interior shows off bone-white "seas" of salt flats, herds of wild camels grazing roadside, "road trains" (trucks of three or four trailers), and the sparse cafes that handle basic needs for travelers. A detour to Kings Canyon for an overnight adds yet another dimension.

Kings Canyon is about 300 kilometers north of Uluru or about a four-hour drive. It comprises part of Watarrka National Park, home to the aboriginal Luritja tribe for over 20,000 years. Its soaring, red sandstone canyon walls tower three hundred yards straight up; think three football fields, end on end. Along the top, a six-kilometer walk traces the perimeter of this gorgeous canyon.

Note: The Outback is desert which means that Australian summer temperatures (December-February) top 100 degrees Farenheit routinely. The "rim walk" is a serious physical undertaking not appropriate during the summer months. All walkers should carry water with them, wear appropriate clothing, and check the temperature before starting out. Since the path is narrow in some places, the park rangers encourage walking in one direction only.

Your rim walk begins with an ascent of about five hundred steps. If you are moderately fit, you can make the climb without too much difficulty, although the local name for this rise is Heartbreak Hill. Once at the top, the hard part is over, and you can start to savor the breathtaking views over the landscape. The red, craggy rocks on all sides will underpin everything you see and do for the next few hours.

As you traverse the rim, at times you'll find yourself on a simple path, looking out on a big view of the surrounding and largely empty Outback landscape. At other times, you'll walk over flat open areas with views within the canyon. You'll encounter teenagers bounding along. You might see a family with young kids picnicking in the shade under a rocky overhang. The sandstone rock shows many faces, jutting in and out, hanging over you, spreading in broad plateaus, and providing lookout points suitable for rest and contemplation. It is eternal and vast.

As you progress, if you miss your StairMaster, consider dropping down to visit the Garden of Eden, a perpetual watering hole with a small bridge across it. Once you've finished your R&R in this lush green spot, you can exit from there or climb back up to the rim.

You should allot about four hours to do the walk without any lengthy stops. The descent is much easier than the initial climb, but you certainly wouldn't want to do it in the gloaming, where a missed step could result in a twisted ankle or worse.

Fans of the movie *Priscilla, Queen of the Desert* will recognize the rim walk from the final triumphant scenes in the film. Yes, they really did haul "her" up there—and, of course, all the camera equipment necessary to capture it on film. It must have been a major undertaking!

In the park nearby, you can spend the night at a comfortable resort with a bar, making a special evening out of it with dinner under the moon. However, be sure to dress warmly for the evening. Like all deserts, Outback temperatures drop significantly after sundown.

SYDNEY HARBOUR BRIDGE CLIMB

Sydney, Australia, boasts several world-famous icons, most notably the sail-like structure of the Sydney Opera House. The Opera House sits flush with the beautiful waters of Sydney Harbour, described as the most perfect harbor in the world.

With a metropolitan population of almost five million people living on both sides of the harbor, Sydney needs bridges, and in 1932, the Sydney Harbour Bridge came into service, carrying car, rail, bike, and pedestrian traffic. The steel-through construction uses a central arch that is the biggest in the world, soaring 440 feet into the sky.

You can climb it!

Perhaps you think, "That must be scary," or "I could never do that." "I have a fear of heights, so that's not for me." "That must be incredibly dangerous," or "Only daredevils would want to do that." In fact, it's not that scary. You CAN do it. It's not dangerous. About four million people have climbed it since 1998, most of whom were not daredevils. Note: *If you have a crippling fear of heights, it would not be appropriate. However, if your fear of heights is in the normal range, you will most likely be absolutely fine.*

As a BridgeClimber, you will meet next to the bridge to receive a briefing, take a Breathalyzer test, and change into climbing gear supplied by the BridgeClimb company. In the briefing room, you will test-climb two short ladders. If you can climb them without difficulty and you pass the Breathalyzer test, you will be accepted for the climb.

In the locker room, you must park your personal items in a locker. No phones, no earrings, no watch, nothing that can come loose can go with you. BridgeClimb will make sure that you cannot be a danger to yourself or others while on the bridge.

Now, you'll don a jumpsuit, complete with an attached pullover in case you get cold, a hankie for your personal needs, and, most importantly, a safety harness with pull-rings. Finally, you'll pop on a set of headphones so that you can hear your group leader over the noise of the wind.

Once you understand the safety system, you'll understand why four million people have done this safely over the years. When you begin the BridgeClimb, the safety harness pull-ring will attach to a cable that runs inside a track that begins at the base of the arch. The cable track continues up the side of the arch, across the top of the span, and back down the other side. In order, everyone in your group will attach to that cable. Once the cable connects into the steel track, it cannot disengage until you come back down the other side of the arch.

First, you traverse the trestle catwalks that connect the steel superstructure to land. The catwalks sit above the roadway and if you want to look down, you will see eight lanes of cars zipping the locals from one side of the harbor to the other. Occasionally, trains will rumble through with a lot of noise that vanishes as quickly as it comes.

On the other side of the catwalk, you'll find a few short ladders. Up you climb to the beginning of the arch. The arch walkway sits well away from the very edge of the bridge. That's why it's not as scary as it

sounds. It does slope upward, but there are bracing boards all along for more secure footing. Your trusty group guide will stop every now and then to explain unbelievable facts about the bridge, to let you rest, and to take in the increasingly astonishing views.

Shortly, you will find yourself standing in the sky, overlooking one of the most beautiful cities in the world. There's that iconic Opera House! There's the city center! There's the Taronga Zoo on the far side of the harbor! What a view. What an experience!

When the guide asks you if you'd like to make a short video at the top, say yes. It will be waiting for you when you're back down on the ground, in the shop. I guarantee you that your video will capture you in an exhilarated frame of mind. It's a wonderful memento.

And now, with your group, you will cross over the top of the arch and begin the descent. Again, the bracing boards provide additional stability as you come back down to earth. Eventually, you'll come to a matching pair of those short ladders. Climb down. Cross those catwalks to solid land again and you're done!

WITH AN ABORIGINAL ELDER

The Australian aboriginal tribes have treated Uluru (Ayers Rock) as a sacred place for thousands of years, long predating the arrival of western settlers. Once you see the giant outcropping in person, it's easy to understand why. Unlike its image on a thousand calendars and tour itineraries, Uluru is not a solid monolith. Up close, you can see that the giant outcropping sports numerous rock faces, caves, crevices, overhangs, and other geological features. Your tour guide can show you cave paintings there, thousands of years old.

Your visit to Uluru may feature an overnight at the Ayers Rock resort which offers a variety of accommodations at different price points, all with different names but operated by the same company. Onsite, you can participate in several tours exploring aspects of the area, including insights into the native culture. In particular, this is a great place to learn about aboriginal art from a local tribal elder and then, try your hand at it.

Originally, aboriginal art was created directly in the soil and then smoothed over afterwards. The art served as a temporary channel to connect people to long-standing rituals through sacred images and body paint. The artists outlined the designs with circles and then added dots outside the circles. Many of the images were closely guarded secrets unseen and not understood by people outside of the tribe, whether Westerners or members of other tribes. Dots helped disguise the symbols and keep them secret.

Aboriginal art always tells a story, using symbols to portray interaction with the land, local beliefs, and important events. Sometimes, the artist seems to look down upon the land from above as he or she interprets their Dreamtime or Creationtime or harks back to ancestral and familiar spirits.

Every afternoon at the Ayers Rock resort, a local elder will explain the principles of aboriginal dot art to interested visitors. She will explain the traditions that inform cultural and spiritual life of the local people and the tools that men and women use in their daily lives. As she demonstrates how a dot painting grows from a blank canvas, she might actually draw her own painting in the soil, as this was the original medium of dot art. She will explain the meaning of the symbols she includes, their connection to her own life, to each other, and to the larger story she is telling

The simplicity of the dot paintings created by the artists is misleading. You may think that a child could easily create something similar. Not so. This misperception rapidly becomes apparent as you start your own dot painting.

First, you must decide what story you will tell and how you will tell it. Perhaps you will want to demonstrate a timeline of your life. Perhaps you will focus on a significant event or events. Perhaps you will want to portray your relationship to your family or your own circle of life. You can choose anything.

Once you decide on your story, it's time to select the symbols you will incorporate into the image. The local people use symbols to represent tools used in daily life, people alone or in groups, the concept of travel with a resting place, and natural phenomena like rainbows or the sun and stars. You can choose to either adopt one of these traditional symbols or make your own.

Of course, the relationship between your symbols is essential to your story and the dots will connect them. Dots can also be used for decoration or for filling in blank spaces.

By the time you are halfway through your own painting, you will undoubtedly recognize the complexity of this unique art form. Have fun with your creativity; you can take it home with you. But the one you'll probably want to hang on the wall is the one you buy from a true aboriginal artist.

AUSTRIA

VIENNA
WATTENS

A VIENNESE BALL

Cue the orchestra. Throw on your ballgown, tuxedo, or business suit. Summon up your inner Cinderella and prepare for a special evening.

The Viennese know how to waltz. They do it really well, and they do it a lot. In fact, they've been dancing the night away since 1815, over 200 years and counting. Every year, the major Ball Season occurs between New Year's Eve and Ash Wednesday when this former imperial capital hosts about four hundred events. Many of them are sponsored by professions such as lawyers, confectioners, pharmacists, doctors, and coffeehouse owners. The list goes on. The locations vary, but you might find yourself twirling away inside the Imperial Palace, the Hofburg. The coffeehouse owners boast that their ball is the only one that can use all of the Hofburg Ballrooms, including the refurbished Redoutensäle and the elegant roof foyer with its view over nighttime Vienna.

My favorite is the Fête Impériale which occurs in June and is the only ball scheduled for the summer. The Fête Impériale serves as a benefit to safeguard the future of the famous white stallions of the Spanish Riding School, the Lipizzaners. You, too, can join the cream of Viennese Society at the stunning Spanish Riding School performance hall in the Hofburg on that one special night.

The arena is an elegant space with boxes for spectators and chandeliers above a sand floor. But on this night, it transforms into a fairyland with a black and white dance floor, a full orchestra, and dining tables. A myriad of multicolored spotlights play over the floor and the walls, while a luscious soundtrack of classic waltz music fills your ears.

Because the horses themselves have gone on their annual summer vacation to Pilsen in the Czech countryside, the courtyard around which their stalls are arranged provides a second dance area—this one with a rock band. Whether you want to waltz or do the twist, you'll find your tribe—and, of course, you can wander back and forth between the two areas.

While you do so, look for a small plaque on the wall noting the role that General George S. Patton played in the closing days of World War II to safeguard the Lipizzaners. It's a small but interesting tale about a cavalryman general who made sure the white stallions survived.

Perhaps you're concerned that your waltz skills need some brushing up? No problem. The Elmayer Dance School in downtown Vienna will happily give you a one-hour lesson in advance. Even a novice can learn enough to venture out on the dance floor.

What about hair and make-up? No problem. My favorite hotel will arrange for an in-room session to suit your needs.

Perhaps you'd like to arrive in style if you're going to spend an evening at the Palace? Hire a horse-drawn carriage to transport you from your hotel. As you clip-clop over the cobblestones to the palace entrance in your finery, the magic will take over. The ball host may greet you outside the Palace door in a receiving line when the "entrance" begins at 7:30 pm. Photographers will capture the A-listers while you wait.

Traditions continue inside and it's best to find a seat in the spectator boxes for the formal program. You'll hear some speeches from the Ball organizers, followed by a special introductory performance. Finally, the entrance of debutantes and their escorts will occur, and the young people will fill the floor for a first dance in a swirl of black and white tuxedos and ballgowns. Afterwards, with the words *Alles Walzer* ("Everything is Waltz"), the floor will open to everyone, probably around 9 pm. A formal "quadrille" occurs at midnight and the last waltz is usually around 4 am. It's a late night.

The dance floor is a vast space, of course, since it's designed for horses to perform in. When you sally forth onto that beautiful floor, with the glorious waltz music swelling around you, the multicolored lights playing over the crowd, and with happy people dancing and twirling on every side, your inner Cinderella/Prince Charming will emerge, guaranteed! Since the champagne flows freely all night, the whirling and twirling may internalize at a certain point, all to your benefit.

Happily, the tickets to these balls are not exorbitantly expensive—about EUR 100 per person, and students can buy a ticket for half-price. The extras of course can add up, but for a once-in-a-lifetime experience, you might just want to do it up right.

THE THIRD MAN TOUR

Calling all movie buffs. Fans of the iconic film *The Third Man* can easily retrace the locales known to Harry Lime and his partners in crime.

Director Carol Reed made *The Third Man* in 1948 when the scars of World War II were still raw and obvious in many European cities, epitomized by piles of rubble from the shelling and fighting. Vienna was no different. All these years later, the signs of war have long vanished except for the occasional bullet holes sighted in old buildings. Happily, the iconic sights of the city that defined the movie are easy to find.

If you've never seen the movie, watch it now. It holds up beautifully and tells a captivating story. Orson Welles stars as Harry Lime, a small-time racketeer profiting from the misery of the post-war era. His childhood friend (Joseph Cotten) arrives in Vienna to take a job that his friend Harry has promised him. Much to his dismay, he discovers that Harry Lime has been killed in a car accident that very afternoon. I won't say more about the plot to avoid any spoilers, but Graham Greene wrote an excellent story.

One of the most memorable scenes takes place at the giant ferris wheel in the city's Prater Park. The *Riesenrad* (dubbed "that big wheel" by Joseph Cotten's character) continues to revolve today, giving visitors a glorious bird's-eye view of Vienna and the adjacent Danube River. Notably, as you buy your tickets for the ride, you'll see Orson Welles's face painted in a small mural next to the ticket booth. Harry Lime lives on! To add authenticity to your "flight," book a Harry Lime dinner. That's easiest done for small groups, but individuals can book a single spot on the third day of each month. The event offers a Harry Lime cocktail and an Allies starter plate.

The *Third Man*-o-philes might want to see a bit of the Vienna sewer system. Again, no spoilers here, but the sewers are almost their own character in the film. You can tour them today, and they have an interesting past and present. Well-maintained walkways allow you access to numerous parts of the sewers in the city center. The sound of rushing water all around you will fill your ears while the city of Vienna pays homage to the film with mood lighting and Orson Welles's face projected on the walls.

Other notable locations in the film include *Josefsplatz* and a remaining elevated section of the old city's walls, the *Molker Bastei* in front of the University of Vienna. As in many historic European cities, when attacks from invaders died down centuries ago, the town fathers deemed the walls unnecessary and destroyed much of them. However, several sections remain, including this one. The Viennese always liked going for walks "up above" for the views and Ludwig von Beethoven actually lived here from time to time until 1814.

Joseph Cotten's character stays at the iconic Sacher Hotel, located next to the Vienna State Opera House. Graham Greene lived on the top floor while he wrote the treatment that became the movie, and The Sacher cossets its guests to this day. Even if you don't book a room there, you might want to peek inside to see its gracious reception room, and you should definitely sample the famous Sacher Torte.

You will need transportation to visit the central cemetery, featured at the beginning and the end of *The Third Man*. You'll find it in Simmering, about fifteen minutes south of the city center by car. Many famous people are buried here, including Beethoven, Brahms, Schubert, and Johann Strauss. (No, Mozart is not buried here. He was thrown into a pauper's grave at his death, although the cemetery now features a monument to him.)

Intrepid explorers can find most of these locations on their own, very easily and for free. But several tour companies offer *The Third Man* tours as well as separate tours of the sewer system to add additional insight and background. Because the movie still resonates all these years later, you can even visit a museum dedicated to the film.

The museum displays artifacts from the movie but also presents meaningful commentary about postwar Vienna and postwar life for the people who lived through those chaotic days. With Germany's surrender in 1945, the four victorious allies (The United States, Great Britain, France, and the Soviet Union) divided Austria and, separately, Vienna, into four zones, each administered by a different country. Not until 1955 did Austria and Vienna revert to independent status.

The Third Man captures this tumultuous postwar era and its repercussions while presenting a riveting personal story that anyone can follow. For Vienna visitors who haven't seen the movie but want to, it continues to play routinely at a local cinema, the Burg Kino, right in the city center, on a set schedule.

SWAROVSKI CRYSTAL WORLDS

If you've ever visited Vienna or Austria (or your parents did), chances are you acquired a small Swarovski crystal, perhaps in the shape of a porcupine or a duck. Not too expensive. Pretty. Sparkly. Sound familiar?

Swarovski has been creating crystalline works of art for more than one hundred years. When they got to their centennial, they decided to go big to celebrate. Really big. It's called Crystal Worlds.

The first thing you'll meet is a botanical green giant. He covers the side of a hill, and his mouth serves to launch an impressive waterfall. As light plays through the falling water, you'll understand how important rays of light are to everything that Swarovski does, whether on a tiny porcupine or a gigantic Hall of Wonders.

Inside, the Blue Hall introduces you to a different way of seeing some famous pieces of art. Here you can enjoy modern, light oriented interpretations of Dali's *Persistence of Memory* and Andy Warhol's *Gems*.

Want to see a snowscape from a new angle? Check out the Silent Light chamber and its crystal tree. In 2020, this sparkling artwork got a new home in a poetic snow installation, raising questions about the transience and fragility of nature in the world around us. Note: *bring a sweater because the temperature can get as low as 14 °C.*

The Ice Passage introduces an audio-visual element. This vast hall appears deserted at first, but as you place your foot on the floor, your tracks start to appear. Your own tracks will trace your path as you move through. The lights also trace these tracks, giving you, the traveler, glances into the surrounding world of glistening ice. The further you go and the more people who go with you, the brighter and more luminescent the surroundings become. Meanwhile, the tracks on the floor appear denser. Each step you take creates alarming creaking and crackling in the virtual ice. Careful: Don't fall in.

Remember Buckminster Fuller's Geodesic Dome? Swarovski offers a Crystal Dome for your delight. A geodesic dome uses the mathematical principle designating the shortest path between two points on a curved surface. Geodesic domes are very stable, and the Crystal Dome consists of 595 mirrors that create a special depth effect, making you feel like you are inside a crystal. Eight "spy mirrors" reflect art objects by various artists. Appropriately, Brian Eno orchestrated a New Age soundtrack to round out the experience.

Lest you think the artists have done all the work for you, you'll need to stop in at the Studio Job Wunderkammer (the Chamber of Wonder). Building on the old concept of a small curiosity cabinet that holds a collection of scientific exhibits, the Chamber of Wonder invites the visitor to experience colors, shapes, compositions, and concepts on an individual basis. There are no corners in this room, but you'll find movement, music, reflections, and allusions to modern society here.

Fernando Romero's installation *El Sol* (or The Sun) draws on 2,880 custom-made Swarovski crystals, exploring our relationship with the sun (pretty fundamental to us all). This structure is exactly one billion times smaller than the sun itself. At the heart of the artwork lies a sphere of LEDs. The inner facets of the precisely cut crystals split the light in such a way that it creates a dynamic surface reminiscent of the sun.

Mr. Romero sought to pay homage to the Aztec and Mayan pyramids of his native Mexico, while using design and development techniques of the modern world.

Seventeen separate chambers and art works make up Crystal Worlds, and that's just inside. Outdoors, the gardens combine light, crystals, and the natural world to create a mirror pool, a crystal cloud, and climbing structures for the young and the young at heart. Art installations populate the extensive landscape, continuing to tickle your senses and stimulate your brain.

CAMBODIA

SIEM REAP

PHARE CIRCUS PERFORMANCE

Visitors flock to Siem Reap these days to goggle at the incredible temples of the area, including Angkor Wat. Since thirty-five temples dot the surrounding countryside in all stages of maintenance and disrepair, you can channel your inner Lara Croft to your heart's content—and then head back to relax poolside at one of the great local hotels. Inexpensive restaurants abound for dinner, and you can buy some beautiful handicrafts made locally. You'll find exquisite silk clothing, table linens, and decorative items, intricate wood carvings, jewelry, and temple rubbings, among other traditional items. It all combines to make a terrific experience. Any guidebook can describe these options.

But add one thing more! Suspend your sophistication and attend a wonderful local performance at Phare Circus. This simple one-ring circus will enchant even the most worldly, jaded traveler.

After an early dinner in town, hop in a tuk-tuk for a short ride to the simple pink circus tent on the outskirts of town. Or arrive between 5 and 8 pm to sample street food from local chefs.

Make your way inside to find rough wooden benches arranged in tiers around a simple circus ring on the floor. You and your 329 fellow spectators will enjoy a great view near the amazing performers.

And here they come—a procession of Cambodian teenagers who will entertain you with music, acting, acrobatics, juggling, and other traditional circus arts. Spoiler alert: You won't see elephants or lion tamers at Phare Circus.

What will you see?

At first, the performers may seem amateurish, and you may wonder if this is a just a worthy kids' performance. But over the course of the hour-long show, the difficulty of the circus feats increases, and the skill and dexterity of the young artists becomes more and more impressive. You'll watch them demonstrate incredible balance, acrobatics, strength, elegance, and grace, always with youthful energy and smiling faces. By the time the performance has ended, you will have fallen in love with these performers' enthusiasm, skill, and heart.

And just what is Phare circus exactly? In the Cambodian town of Battambang, many local children are born into extreme poverty. Others lose their parents and are threatened with bare survival on the streets and a lifetime of need. Phare, a local nonprofit, identifies these kids and encourages them to attend school and acquire professional training in visual arts (illustration, painting, graphic design, and animation), as well as performing arts such as theater, music, dance, and circus. More than 1,200 students attend the public school daily, of which 500 participate in the vocational arts training programs. It is all free. Phare circus provides most of the funding for the school through sales of tickets, food, and merchandise.

When the performance ends, you will find yourself clapping and cheering as the teenagers take their well-earned bows. When the lights come on, the kids will remain in the ring, and you are free to make your way down onto the tent floor. Here you can meet the performers, congratulate them, thank them, take their pictures, have your picture taken with your favorite artist or two, and bask in simple and spontaneous friendship. Smiles abound on every side. Don't be surprised if you find yourself wanting to support Phare and the wonderful work that they do to change young lives.

CANADA

DRUMHELLER, ALBERTA
NIAGARA ESCARPMENT
PRINCE EDWARD ISLAND
VANCOUVER ISLAND

DINOSAUR FOSSIL HUNT

Have you ever noticed how many fossils carry the title "Dinosaur *albertosaurus,*" where the word dinosaur is replaced by the type: *Stegosaurus* or *Tyrannosaurus*, etc.? Those classification names derive from a valley near Drumheller in Alberta, Canada, a treasure trove for fossil hunters. You'll find Drumheller about 100 miles north and east of Calgary.

Humans remain continually fascinated by the dinosaurs of prehistoric times. We see their skeletons in museums of natural history. We write about them in elementary school. We each have our favorite type and our enthusiasm tends to last into adulthood. As a result, moviemakers continue to make blockbuster films about them.

In 1884, a man named J.B. Tyrrell arrived in Drumheller looking for coal. He found it, but he also found a dinosaur skull; that dinosaur became known as Albertosaurus Sarcophagus (or "flesh-eating lizard from Alberta"). Ever since, "Dinosaur Valley" has gradually given up hundreds of dinosaur fossils which end up in museums all over the world. The valley has produced over 350 good skeletons, with the oldest bones dating back 110 million years. Scientists have identified sixty to seventy different dinosaur types in the area. Clearly, Drumheller attracted many dinosaur residents back in the day.

The valley, originally lush and wet, provided an environment where dinosaurs could dine and flourish. After the dinosaurs died out, sediments from the rivers covered their remains, preserving them in the mud. When glaciers receded at the end of the Ice Age, they left behind lakes and the dry Red Deer River Valley as it is known today.

A ninety-minute drive from Calgary to Drumheller will take you through the Alberta Badlands, a dusty, desiccated, brown, empty landscape. As you approach this remote town, you'll know you've arrived when you see the gigantic *Tyrannosaurus rex* greeting you at the town entrance.

Head first to the outstanding Royal Tyrrell Museum, the only museum in the world dedicated to paleontology. Its first-rate collection will keep any dinosaur enthusiast occupied for several hours. Skeletons abound, including a terrific *Tyrannosaurus rex* and the ever-popular triceratops. In addition, you'll find wonderful exhibits recreating the world in which the dinosaurs lived. Many of them were invertebrates (lacking a backbone) and some of them are probably unknown to you. By the time you've finished your tour, you will know a LOT about dinosaurs.

And now, you can head up into Alberta's sandy landscape to see what you can find. The museum offers a program called Dinosite in which participants can search for fossils and see real dinosaur remains still in the ground in a ninety-minute, three-kilometer hike through the badlands.

For individuals, it's important to understand the rules, enforced with significant fines for violators. Alberta's laws protect its dinosaurs, and you must understand what you may and what you may NOT do.

As a casual visitor, you may see if you can find fossils on the surface of the ground on Provincial Crown Land only. Notably, the land immediately around the museum remains off limits to fossil hunters. In addition, you may not dig for fossils without a permit issued through the museum. Only professional paleontologists may excavate fossils.

If you find a fossil, know that you may NOT keep it yourself. In the spirit of advancing human knowledge, you should:

1. Photograph it and note any visible features (for scale, include a coin or pen).
2. Locate it on a map using permanent landmarks (use GPS if available).
3. Leave it buried. If the fossil is lying on the surface of the ground, bring it to the museum.
4. Report the find. Email the head technician at the museum at tyrrell.fossilreport@gov.ab.ca. Include your first and last name, telephone number, email address, the location where you found the fossil (with GPS coordinates, if possible), and a photograph of the fossil.

What might you find on your surface search? Dinosaur teeth. Dinosaur bones. Dinosaur poop. The sandstone landscape continues to yield up its secrets. You'll have a truly great show-and-tell item when you get home.

THE WELLAND CANAL

The Niagara Escarpment, which includes world-famous Niagara Falls, presents a formidable obstacle to navigation. Imagine that you need to transport your goods to the interior of North America, whether Canada or the United States. Down the St. Lawrence Seaway and the St. Lawrence River aiming for Lake Ontario and parts west, you come. Smooth sailing until... Niagara Falls. Problem. Big problem. Two hundred fifty feet of a big problem.

Starting in the early 1800s, various industrialists recognized that they needed to create a way to bypass Niagara Falls for commercial purposes. The Erie Canal to the south had simplified transit from east to west within the US. However, British interests in Canada feared that they needed a counterpart on their side of the border to compete. One, two, and three versions of the canal were dug, locks were installed, portage over small roads was included, trains were involved, channels widened, locks were removed, and in the end, a fourth version of the Welland Canal took shape in the 1920s.

Because of the Welland Canal, cargo can travel from the Atlantic Ocean down the St. Lawrence River into Lake Ontario and then bypass Niagara Falls on its way into Lake Erie and on through the Great Lakes Waterway, thirteen hundred miles into the interior of the continent. About three thousand ships use the canal each year. What a great role it plays in the commerce of both the US and Canada!

Interestingly, various acts of sabotage have occurred from almost its first days. Various malcontents have sought to blow up the locks, but luckily the damage was minor. The most recent action, known as "The Von Papen Plot," took place during World War I. In April 1916, a United States federal grand jury issued an indictment against Franz von Papen, Captain Hans Tauscher, Captain Karl Boy-Ed, Constantine Covani, and Franz von Rintelen on charges of plotting to blow up the Welland Canal. Von Papen eluded punishment at the time, having been expelled from the US several months previously for alleged earlier acts of espionage and attempted sabotage. Von Papen remained under indictment on these charges until he became Chancellor of Germany in 1932, at which time the charges were dropped.

Today, you can travel on a small cruise ship from Montreal to Lake Michigan with a wonderful transit through the eight locks of the Welland Canal. It takes about seventeen hours to traverse the eight locks and, during that time, your boat will rise or fall 326 feet. Most of the locks cover about 750 feet but Lock 8 (the southernmost one) consists of one lock connected to another lock connected to a third lock, stretching 1,150 feet. As your boat exits one lock, it enters the next.

You'll watch huge tankers float by in the opposite direction. Very serious, very large mechanisms activate to stabilize those giant ships while they're in the lock, and you'll have a front row seat. There's something magical about watching the basic laws of nature slowly and gracefully reposition each boat, exactly as needed. It's a leisurely pursuit for sure. Whether you linger at the prow or the stern of your own craft, the power of the water rushing in or out of the gates will command attention. Slowly you'll rise from the bottom of the steep walls or inexorably sink into the depths.

Of course, the schedule doesn't necessarily match daylight hours. While the rest of the world sleeps snugly at home, you'll watch the dock guys bring the ships into the lock(s) in the dark. Bright lights flood the scene. The dock guys are close enough that you can talk to them. Ask them some questions about how it all works. They're pretty friendly.

And then you float away.

Private watercraft can also transit the Welland Canal, but a few guidelines are in order. The Canal closes from December to mid-April when bad weather and ice pose a danger to ships. In general, the locks operate from 7 am to 7 pm, but commercial traffic takes priority. There are tolls for each lock and a "discount" for using all eight. Crew requirements for passage on the Welland Canal are dependent on the direction of travel. Northbound boats require a minimum of three crew members and southbound require two crew members. You'll find that participating in an organized cruise between Montreal and a port city on one of the Great Lakes will take much less toll on your body than tying up and untying from all those locks.

Various small ships offer this itinerary, and you'll get a day at Niagara Falls, too. The cabins tend toward the miniscule, but you probably won't spend much time in the cabin. You'll enjoy gorgeous scenery all around you and downright fascinating mechanisms in the canal itself.

ON THE TRAIL OF ANNE OF GREEN GABLES

For generations of girls, Prince Edward Island (P.E.I.) has meant one thing: *Anne of Green Gables.* Lucy Maud Montgomery's 1908 novel about the redheaded orphan girl, Anne Shirley, continues to enchant; over 50 million copies of the book have been sold. Over the years, numerous films and TV series have portrayed its plucky heroine and in our modern age, her indomitable spirit resonates widely.

P.E.I. is an island (as its name suggests) but today a bridge connects it with Nova Scotia. Arrival by car is definitely easier than in Anne's lifetime. Happily, major cruise lines often include the port city of Charlottetown on New England itineraries, making an "Anne Day" a breeze.

The island sees many visitors, but the essential landscape that Anne inhabited remains unchanged. The dunes along the ocean, the rolling green hills, the wide expanse of sea and sky, and the gentle pace of life would all be familiar to the heroine of a hundred years ago.

The Anne of Green Gables trail concentrates in and around Cavendish on the north shore of the island. You can start your day with a stop at the Visitors Center in Charlottetown to pick up a map identifying the main sites important to Anne's character and to author Lucy Maud Montgomery. You can visit Montgomery's birthplace, Montgomery's adult home, Green Gables Heritage Place, the Haunted Wood, Green Gables House, and Lovers' Lane on a Cavendish walking tour.

If you arrive with a car, you should park at Green Gables Heritage Place rather than at Montgomery Park. From Green Gables Heritage Place, you can walk through Lovers' Lane to the Haunted Wood and Cavendish.

Montgomery was born in Clifton (near Cavendish) and lived her early life there in a small house. Her widowed father moved out to Alberta when she was seven, leaving her in the care of her grandparents in Cavendish. She spent a lonely childhood, relying on imaginary friends and often dreamed about becoming a writer. A solitary being, she found inspiration in a nearby wood which she termed the Haunted Forest. Young Anne Shirley often describes the wood as a place of deep mystery and spirits.

The house at Green Gables Heritage Place inspired the original *Anne of Green Gables* story. Yes, the gables (the house wall that meets a pitched roof) are green. You can easily imagine the young orphan coming to live here with Matthew and Marilla Cuthbert (who wanted a boy to help on the farm, as all devoted readers of the story are well aware.) The house retains period décor and upstairs you can even see Anne's dress "with puffed sleeves." You can feel the aura of the story and Anne Shirley very strongly here.

Nearby, you'll encounter the Balsom Hollow Trail which includes "Lovers' Lane," a section of the trail to which Montgomery gave that name. This easy loop passes through a lovely verdant forest before connecting to the town of Avonlea.

In the town of Cavendish, look for Montgomery's burial spot in the town cemetery. Although the author moved to Toronto when she married (in her late 30s), she was interred in the town that the world most associates with her.

Close to Cavendish in Park Corner, you will find the Anne of Green Gables museum, a privately owned home belonging to Montgomery's cousin's family. The author spent many happy hours here and she even married in the house. You'll see the same organ and furnishings in the parlor that Montgomery saw at her wedding. Caution: the museum operators have bestowed a strong commercial element on the house with numerous Anne-related items for purchase on-site.

One final note: *If you are looking for the town of Avonlea (as in Anne of Avonlea), Montgomery invented Avonlea, but she based her story on Cavendish.*

ORCA WHALE WATCH

Vancouver Island sits just off the west coast of North America, between Vancouver and Seattle. The scenery grants you dramatic views. You can hop a hydrofoil from Seattle or take a leisurely and lovely four-hour ferry ride through the San Juan Islands from Vancouver. Victoria Airport provides connections by air, as well.

The small city of Victoria boasts a charming waterfront, the iconic, rambling Fairmont Empress hotel, and some nice little restaurants to enjoy. A typical excursion highlights Butchart Gardens, constructed over the remnants of a former limestone quarry outside of town. But Vancouver Island also gives visitors access to orca whale watching.

Several groups of so-called killer whales inhabit the cold clear waters around the island, and whale watching tours are readily available from Victoria. There are different size boats to choose from, but you may prefer a Zodiac.

These rigid inflatable boats carry twelve passengers (Zodiac: get it?) and use powerful engines to cover a lot of ground (er, water) in a short amount of time. Better yet, the fresh wind in your face in these open boats means that you probably won't have any issues with seasickness. Although the waters are mostly protected and fairly calm, the Zodiac boats provide another degree of comfort if you're at all worried about a queasy stomach.

When you show up at the dock, the tour operator will outfit you in a water repellent jumpsuit to wear while on the boat. That open format of the Zodiac means there might be some splashing from time to time; the jumpsuit will protect your clothing.

Your boat pilot will then escort you to the pier to board the Zodiac and begin the search for a pod of orcas. These strikingly hued black and white whales move around of course, but your pilot will inevitably find a group of them to observe. Although the chances of finding a pod are close to 100%, most of the companies will invite you back for a second trip if your search comes up empty-handed. Plan for a three-night stay on Vancouver Island to allow for that unlikely event.

From a safe distance, you will watch these magnificent creatures forage, surface, and dive. They are mesmerizing. Perhaps one or more of them will breach, up out of the water, crashing down with a tremendous splash. When an adult male weighs 12,000 pounds, he makes a helluva crash coming back down.

Did you know that an orca dorsal fin towers six feet high? And there's a lot more whale below that fin.

Your pilot will make sure that you get close enough to enjoy their incredible beauty but far enough away to remain safe at all times. You don't ever want to get between a mother and a calf, of course, which is why you want to go whale-watching with an experienced and reputable outfit.

The babies' coloration is more of tan and black, not turning white until about a year later. That makes it easy to spot a newborn. The mother will have carried the developing calf for about 17 months. At an average of 400 pounds at birth, I'm sure that mama is always happy to let that baby go.

It's true that there are whale watching tours throughout the world. Grey whales, humpbacks, blue whales, minkes, and myriad other cetacean species all inhabit different waters. But some of those waters, particular open ocean, can be very rough, making for a less than optimal experience.

In addition, environmental concerns about whale watching expeditions have led to a code of conduct in recent years to minimize the impact of large-scale tourism on whale populations. You can check if your planned whale watching company observes these procedures. Look for guidelines pledging:

- Minimizing speed/"No wake" speed
- Avoiding sudden turns
- Minimizing noise
- Not pursuing, encircling, or coming in between whales
- Approaching animals from angles where they will not be taken by surprise

Assuming that your tour operator routinely abides by these strictures, sign up and have fun!

The calmness of the waters near Vancouver Island, the dramatic coloration of the orcas, and the availability of the Zodiac boats all combine to give you terrific whale-watching here.

CHILE

PATAGONIA
VALPARAISO

CAVE OF THE MYLODON

The magnificence of Patagonia is hard to overstate. The soaring peaks of Torres del Paine National Park, the dramatic marine glaciers, and the confluence of mountains, lakes, and waterfalls all combine to make this region of Chile one of the most spectacular on our planet.

At peak times of year, you can fly nonstop to Puerto Natales, a convenient base for exploring the landscape around you. This small oasis at the edge of the National Park hosts myriad companies offering tours in and around the park. Sooner or later, someone will mention the Cave of the Mylodon.

What's that? Never heard of a Mylodon? Neither had anyone else until the late 1890s when German explorer Hermann Eberhard discovered the remains of one in a giant cave nearby. After a lot of excitement and heartfelt searches for the elusive creature, eventually scientists determined that the Mylodon had lived about 10,000 years ago!

You can certainly drive to the cave, just fifteen miles from Puerto Natales. However, since the cave sits empty now, take a bike or a hiking tour of the area to channel the prehistoric world. The tours begin in Puerto Natales with transport to the cave area. Usually, you will visit not only the Cave of the Mylodon but several other giant caves, as well as the Devil's Chair rocky outcropping. Although the landscape in the area is primarily flat, some of the bike paths are rough in parts and can challenge rusty bike skills.

As you approach the Cave of the Mylodon, you'll see large silhouettes of other extinct species such as saber-toothed tigers and miniature horses, remains of which have also been found in the cave. The cut-outs will help orient you to the scale of these ancient beasts. The Mylodon itself resembled a giant sloth and stood over ten feet tall on its hind legs, with a strong kangaroo-like tail. Cool!

The size of the cave's gaping mouth reflects the work of thousands of years of strong winds off the local lake, carving ceaselessly into the face of the giant rock. Since the discovery of the Mylodon in the 1890s, explorers have exposed bones of many other creatures inside the cave, as well. It's possible that early humans used the cave to trap animals for their food.

Nearby, you can truck through the weird rock formation known as Devil's Chair. Or you can climb it. From the top, you will get some great views of the surrounding landscape.

Two other smaller caves feature in the immediate area, Cueva del Medio and Cueva Chica. Cueva Chica offers more in-depth exploration but bring a light source with you.

For hikers, your tour will probably include a visit to Cerro Benítez, a good-sized hill which takes about three hours to hike to the top. From the summit, you will see Lake Sofia and Última Esperanza (Last Hope) fjord. Fans of the Andean Condor (the bird with the second largest wingspan anywhere) will have an excellent chance at condor spotting.

This region offers myriad outdoor activities designed to show off the best of Patagonia. A photo safari is a perfectly good way to explore Torres del Paine park by car. But if the Cave of the Mylodon interests you, hiking or biking is the way to go.

STREET ART OF CHILE

An hour west of cosmopolitan Santiago lies the coastal city of Valparaiso, constructed on the steep hills above the major port that serves the nearby capital. Like many port cities, Valparaiso displays a gritty and colorful demeanor, a bit in-your-face. Its history reflects a seesaw of rising and falling fortunes from its eighteenth century status as a major port for European ships to its decline after the creation of the Panama Canal. In recent years, it has once again flourished.

All that trade inevitably brought immigrants from many lands who settled in the city, lending specific neighborhoods different cultural identities. As the population grew, the surrounding hills furnished housing for more and more people. Visitors will see a network of funiculars which transport residents up and down those steep inclines.

Today, parts of the city exhibit a distinct bohemian vibe. Many artists have settled here and have used Valparaiso itself as a canvas for eye-popping street art. The movement dates back to the 1960s when Chilean poet Pablo Neruda encouraged the locals to campaign for government reform by expressing themselves artistically as opposed to putting up political posters.

Add in the protest movement during the Pinochet military rule of the 1970s and 1980s, when political graffiti expanded as a way to express resistance to the authoritarian government. While Chile's political situation has stabilized considerably in recent years, today's artists still blend political commentary with personal expression.

Several of Valparaiso's hills boast graffiti, but Conception Hill displays the greatest concentration of street art. Here, countless murals decorate walls, houses, staircases, and anything else that can be painted. If there's a wall, someone has used it as a canvas. The movement has flowered into block after block of color, form, messaging, and spatial tricks.

The steep hills of the city lend themselves to a whimsical integration of horizontal and vertical dimensions. Be sure to bring along a companion and a camera to capture some of these visual contradictions.

You might find yourself "walking" up a staircase that is simply a wall. Or posing unawares at a ledge with a vertical message below that you will only see once your friend's camera has captured it. Or tilting yourself diagonally to line up with a cityscape oriented that way. Or descending a piano keyboard. Or just marveling at images using a wall three stories high with vibrant, dramatic colors, and startling local imagery.

It's best to hire a guide. They can lead you on a path rich with art through the neighborhood and make sure you see the most interesting and cleverest creations. Sometimes, you must stand in a particular vantage point to appreciate the scene, the art, or even architecture.

Notably, your guide can also drive and park a car in a neighborhood with very steep and narrow streets. Finding a parking spot is not easy and, ideally, your guide will park near the top so

that you walk down the hills as you progress. In addition, a guide can direct you to the funicular where appropriate to avoid a steep uphill climb.

Happily, you'll encounter cafés along the way and an ice cream shop or two to enhance your outing. Set aside a few hours to explore and wander among all the art. The creativity and imagination of what these local artists have wrought is incredible. It's a feast for the eyes and you'll get lots of material for your social media account.

COSTA RICA

MANUEL ANTONIO

CHASING WATERFALLS

Costa Rica lures lots of happy travelers every year to interact with the monkeys in the beautiful national park at Manuel Antonio, walk deep into the rainforest near the Arenal Volcano, and experience the famous zipline "canopy tours" in the place where they were invented. Happily, eco-experiences continue to develop in this friendly vacation spot. Canyoning, kayaking, hiking, surfing, whitewater rafting, and river floats all abound in the hilly terrain and tropical climate.

How about waterfalls? Ready to chase a few along the Pacific coast? You can channel your inner Indiana Jones as you make your way into the jungle to find them.

If you're staying in Manuel Antonio, you'll head south along the coast to Portasol for the first waterfall experience. While not dramatically high, the setting of this little waterfall is particularly lovely. Everything is green and big and alive here amid the dense tropical jungle surrounding you on every side, while water gently spills over the various ledges.

Feel free to take a restorative dip in the pool to cool off and refresh your senses. If you'd prefer a little more adventure, consider jumping. Just how brave are you? The lower jump point is about eight feet up. Braver? Climb up another six feet and take the plunge from fourteen feet. You might want to shield more sensitive parts of the body from the impact.

Next up is Uvita. As you walk through the rainforest, keep your eyes open for monkeys in the trees and other tropical flora and fauna. There's a busy, humming world all around you.

Once you reach Uvita, you'll see a majestic waterfall with a twenty-foot natural waterslide. If you're up for a thrill ride, take the plunge. As you careen down the whitewater chute, get ready for the bottom which vanishes abruptly, launching you on a ten-foot drop into the pool below. Note: *this is not a cruise ship or a waterslide at Disney World. There's not a lifeguard in sight at this "jump-at-your-own-risk" cascade.*

Still not producing enough adrenaline? Wait, there's more...climb up the cliff where you can launch into space on a fourteen-foot fall.

If you fancy yourself a tad mellower, skip the jumps, admire the falling waters, and wade into the tranquil pool, surrounded by the verdant landscape. Afterwards, spend a few minutes with some gentle creatures in the adjacent butterfly garden.

Ready to press on? El Pavón Waterfall lies ahead where you will walk, with a rope, behind the cascading falls into a cave to view the waterfall from inside. Picture yourself inside of a big wave barrel like you might see in those incredible surfing videos on the internet.

Nearby, you'll find beautiful beaches with very few people, perfect for a little R&R after those daring jumps into space.

CROATIA

HVAR

LOST VILLAGES HIKE

Can you say Hvar? No, try again and this time, pronounce the *v* as a *w*. *Hwar*. Now you've got it. Think: dramatic rocky coastline; cobalt blue waters sparkling in the Adriatic Sun; a life and story unto itself.

Historically, Hvar lay at the center of the Adriatic sailing routes, making it a natural trade partner for many, many years. The ancient Greeks founded the colony of Pharos in 384 BC on the site of today's Stari Grad ("Old Town"), making it one of the oldest towns in Europe. Through the era of Venetian dominance over the Adriatic, Hvar rose to importance as a major naval base. Prosperity brought culture and the arts, including one of the first public theaters in Europe, nobles' palaces, and many fine communal buildings.

In the modern world, blessed with gorgeous scenery and lots of good hotels and cafes, Hvar now enjoys a thriving tourist economy, making what had once been a sleepy backwater during the communist era, a fairly busy place in the summer. However, it's easy to leave behind the full hotels and restaurants of this popular island on a day hike to the lost villages.

Two little inland communities once thrived in the hills, but for different reasons were almost completely abandoned. Velo Grablje and Malo Grablje originally served as havens of safety for villagers seeking refuge from pirates preying on the coastal population. Set off on a gentle hike to witness the beauty of traditional architecture and ways of living, as well as learn about medicinal herbs and the Tudor offspring legend.* Seriously!

One hundred years ago, the small town of Velo Grablje served as the center of lavender production for all of Dalmatia (the traditional name of Croatia). However, forest fires and natural emigration gradually led to a decline in population. The young people left for jobs in town or the mainland and, eventually, only a few people still lived there.

In recent years, young relatives of the locals decided to reclaim the abandoned town and, happily, repopulation is well underway. The townspeople now sponsor a Lavender Festival every year in June and July and a few restaurants have opened to provide your midday sustenance, aka lunch.

As you pass through the small village, you'll see simple, traditional stone homes with the red-tiled roofs so typical of the Mediterranean region. Extensive stone walls mark off each farmer's land which hosts all those lavender plants. During lavender season, the endless fields of purple flowers are a feast for the eyes, while in the distance, the sparkling Mediterranean waters offset purple with sun-lit blue. Since you're up in the hills, it's pretty easy to get a great view of it all.

From Velo Grablje, head for Malo Grablje, also abandoned in the 1960s, but sporting a curious and legendary connection to Henry VIII. Following the old trail, retrace the medieval road connecting to Stari Grad on the north side of the island. Starting with approximately twenty long steps, the route continues downhill as a small path for about one and a half kilometers, finishing on a wide, gravelly trail. It should take you about one hour to walk, including short breaks for photo ops.

Malo Grablje dates back to the 1530s. Surrounded by vineyards and olive groves, townspeople cultivated the agricultural plots for wealthy landowners in "town." Over time, the residents grew prosperous from wine production, allowing them to build a water cistern, school, and library, as well as purchase nearby coastal land. Each household received a parcel. By the 1950s and 60s, that coastal land beckoned to the townspeople who responded by packing up and leaving behind their homes.

Like all ghost towns, Malo Grablje is a little bit eerie. The last local dignitary left his small palace in 1968.

Most of the roofs and floors of the nineteenth century stone buildings have collapsed or vanished. The old walls show gaping windows, with a few dangling shutters still in place. Empty terraces connect neighboring dwellings. Scrubby vegetation threatens to take over houses, the church, the bakery, and the other places where humans once lived and flourished. Let your imagination run free while you ponder the passage of years.

Note: the dwellings are unstable, and it would be easy to have an accident should you enter them.

Leaving the ruins, continue through a tunnel to pretty little Milna on the coast where you can enjoy seaside refreshments. It should take about forty-five minutes to get there. After a respite, a small trail will lead you all the way back to Hvar in less than an hour.

Local lore tells of an illegitimate son of Henry VIII who was shipwrecked off the coast of Milna. Upon reaching the shore, he fell in love with a beautiful maiden washing her clothes there. Having married, they founded the village of Malo Grablje, and their offspring resulted in many locals with the last name of Tudor.

EGYPT

LUXOR

SHARM EL SHEIKH AND HURGHADA

HORSEBACK DESERT TOUR

Many people who visit Egypt take a tour that includes a night or two in Cairo, followed by a flight to Luxor to start a three- or four-day Nile cruise that ends in Aswan. Add a short flight to Abu Simbel to goggle at those gigantic pharaoh statues, and a flight back to Cairo. Done! This allows you, the visitor, to see the Pyramids at Giza, the sparkling new Egyptian Museum, the stunning ancient monuments at Luxor, the temples of Karnak, Edfu, and Philae, and maybe even a drive over the High Dam at Aswan.

But if you are exploring independently, consider adding another night in Luxor so that you can experience a desert tour by horseback. Luxor's famous monuments are breathtaking. The endless rows of sphinxes, the massive columns at the Temple of Karnak, and the tombs at the Valley of the Kings are definitely "job number one" for you, the visitor. But aside from the tourism that Luxor offers, rural life outside the town continues to function in very traditional ways, and it's accessible.

You'll need to cross the river (yes, the Nile), and check in at one of the reputable horse stables on the West Bank. The stables typically offer a short,

one-hour ride, a sunset tour and then the four-hour desert tour; that's the one you want.

Off you go into the countryside. As you leave the river, you'll ride through lush sugar cane fields. Considering that Luxor (and much of Egypt) exhibits mostly desert hues of dusty sand, grey rock, and scrubby brush, the emerald-green fields strike a startling contrast to everything else you've seen. Bananas grow nearby and the sight of so much fertile land is a reminder of what the Nile does for Egypt.

As you make your way toward Mount Thebes, you'll pass through traditional mud brick villages. The houses are simple structures, with more prosperous families adding on a second story as they are able. Maybe you'll see a handprint on the wall, symbolizing the five pillars of Islam. If the residents have made the pilgrimage to Mecca, they'll show it.

The farmers will be heading to their fields with their camels for the day's work. Not donkeys. Not pick-up trucks. Camels. This is the Middle East. In the village, the scent of the bakery will reach you before your eyes see it. A tall column of what looks like inflated pillows has just come out of the oven. Soon the air will escape, leaving behind the flat, round pita bread that serves as a staple.

Ducks for sale hang in cages. If school is not in session, friendly children might gaze curiously at you out their door. Their mothers are probably congregating at the village well, drawing the water they need for their day's activities. The glimpse of village life suggests you have gone back in time.

Your horses will be heading for Mount Thebes, the low mountains that host the Valley of the Kings, the Valley of the Queens, and the Valley of the Nobles. Here is the site of King Tut's tomb and those of other ancient local dignitaries. Also, in these hills lies the tomb of Hatshepsut, the only female pharaoh. Yes, there WAS one. She dressed as a man, pasted on a ceremonial beard, and adopted the regalia of the ruler. Her tomb carries an elegance and a grace that speaks to us all these centuries later.

As your horse climbs higher up the mountain, the view is astounding. Let's face it, there are many beautiful views from mountains in the world. But not like this one.

Remember the dusty, dry colors of the desert that I mentioned earlier? That's what surrounds you on the mountain. But behold what you can see from here.

In the foreground, your immediate surroundings: rocks, sand, minimal vegetation. It's a monochrome landscape. Below you, those lush sugar cane fields catch your eye in a wide strip of green. Beyond them, a sliver of blue. That's the Nile. On the far side, you'll see another strip of green. Beyond that, the hues of the Sahara Desert stretch endlessly to the horizon.

This one single vista brings you a dramatic pictorial demonstration of what the Nile means to Egypt. It is everything. Without the Nile, there is no life. There is no Egypt. Desert, green, blue, green, desert.

As you descend the mountain and return to the banks of the Nile, those lush fields will fill your vision with the rich green of sustainable life. The ancient Egyptians lived and died here in just the same way that their descendants do today – except for the big hotels and restaurants, of course!

If you have the time for this journey into rural Egyptian life, you will also feel the warmth and hospitality of the Egyptian people towards friends, towards strangers, towards anyone in need. It is a remarkable and wonderful characteristic of this country and culture.

Tip: *Time your visit for the afternoon, returning to Luxor by felucca at sunset. The full sail billowing out while the colors change around you and the life of the Nile slips by makes for an incredibly evocative moment. The eternity of this ancient waterway can't help but captivate you.*

RED SEA SNORKELING

There's snorkeling. And then there's snorkeling in the Red Sea. The coral reefs of the Red Sea furnish the best snorkeling anywhere in the world. Protection from oceanic currents make the waters calm and warm. These conditions have nourished the development of lush underwater life, including more than two hundred species of corals, over one thousand species of fish, and a thousand kinds of invertebrates. Even if you think you've snorkeled the best in the Pacific, the Caribbean, and the South Pacific, the Red Sea tops them all.

As you paddle along the surface, you might find yourself snorkeling alongside spinner dolphins or green sea turtles or dugongs (like a big manatee). The vast array of sea life includes everything from lionfish to clownfish to moray eels.

Many Egypt-bound visitors have heard of Sharm el Sheikh, the lovely resort at the southeastern tip of the Sinai Peninsula. Although coral reefs pop up right in front of some of the hotels, excursions will offer you even more of the incredible undersea universe that defines the Red Sea.

Snorkel trips from Sharm el Sheikh often head to Ras Mohammad National Park, which encompasses the coral reefs at the southernmost tip of the Sinai Peninsula. As a protected marine reserve, it offers clear waters and numerous sites, as well as two small islands: Tiran and Sanafir. Daytrips to Tiran usually offer two or three stops on and around the island.

Nearby lies Gordon Reef, a seashell-shaped reef known for the wreck of the Lovilla. The hard coral attracts banner fish, parrot fish, cornet fish, and blue-spotted sting rays, as well as manta rays and white-tip sharks.

A little further afield, about a hundred kilometers north, lies Dahab, famous for its blue hole, a vertical 394-foot-deep underwater sinkhole. Snorkelers can explore the coral drop-offs that line the blue hole. You can also snorkel the reef that edges the city (in Mashraba) and at Lagoon Beach. En route to Dahab, you'll pass the canyon where a shallow lagoon lies amid the reef flats, as well as a coral drop-off.

On the western bank of the Red Sea lies Hurghada, another, less fashionable, resort town. It's less tony than Sharm el Sheikh, but it's also less expensive. You can snorkel equally well from Hurghada. You might find your boat parked over a reef that rises from the depths of the sea all the way to just below the surface in a riot of rich colors and coral. Here, again, you'll find yourself in calm protected waters, perfect for those with a nervous stomach.

Near Hurghada, the incredible range of hues in the water itself has few parallels in the world. Because of the widely varied depth of the seafloor offshore, you'll find everything from pea green to light turquoise to inky blue cobalt, all in the same small area.

Hurghada itself has swollen from a small town of 12,000 people in the early 1980s to a bustling resort city of 250,000 souls. Along with that exponential growth, of course, has come hotel construction which has resulted in a decline in the fragile reefs directly in front of the town. However, the bays south of Hurghada still offer an amazing array of snorkel opportunities.

Divers can choose a full day excursion that includes some beach time on Giftun Island or a pure snorkel adventure that might include three stops on quiet island shores as well as anchoring in the middle of the sea. The surrounding waters offer a separate universe of sea life, all in living color. Choose a small boat for the most low-key experience.

ENGLAND

COVENTRY
LIVERPOOL
WARWICK CASTLE

LAND ROVER TEST DRIVE

For those of us residing in urban and suburban areas, our SUVs are a luxury. We commonly see Land Rovers and Range Rovers driving well-maintained roads in densely populated areas. Although the SUV concept allows for off-roading, let's face it: those cars mostly spend their days hauling kids to soccer practice and occasionally loading up for a family trip to the beach.

But once upon a time, in the late 1940s, the British Rover car company set out to design a vehicle to mimic a World War II era jeep. The Scottish designer wanted a car durable enough to trek across the spongy Scottish Highlands. And maybe his farm in Wales.

We all know that the United Kingdom gets a lot of rain. However, it varies and, at times, the ground is bone dry. Often, it's a wet and soggy mess, threatening to suck in and mire anything on wheels in unnegotiable muck. This dream car or truck had to be able to handle anything it came across. In fact, Land Rover has become associated with traversing the trackless plains of Africa under similarly changeable conditions—and a lot fewer roads or even tracks. How many movies have you seen featuring Land Rovers next to lions or giraffes?

But what can a Land Rover really do? You can find out for yourself at the factory in Coventry. Sign up for an Experience Drive and put on your seat belt. Note: *you will be a passenger only, not a driver.*

Once you're safely buckled in, your Experience Driver will turn around and ask, "Ready?" And then you head for the Test Area. No silky paved roads for you! Prepare to jiggle, jostle, bump, jump, and leap forward. Got a back problem? You might want to skip this one.

Your Land Rover will start out bumping along a grassy hillock. It's not a smooth journey. Soon, your driver will start putting this special purpose machine through its paces: a hole in the ground here, a mound there. The Land Rover will take you up VERY, VERY steep hills with shifting gravelly rock underneath. You'll probably find yourself bracing against gravity as you jiggle back down the other side.

Your Land Rover will drive through unstable, sandy areas and always maintain traction. And eventually you'll traverse a boggy mess, full of bottom land with mud, standing water, and uncertain terrain. Surely, you'll get stuck here. Nope. In you slide and out you climb. And then, the most amazing part...

Not all land in the outback or hills of Africa is level for two parallel wheels. You will find yourself on a 45° slope, sideways. Instinctively, you will shift to the higher side to make sure you don't all tip over. Fear not, the Land Rover will not tip. It's designed NOT to tip. Can it go to 50°? Yes, it can.

Interestingly, none of this activity will occur at a fast pace. This is a slow-and-steady-wins-the-race approach. In fact, this Land Rover doesn't even have a brake. It doesn't need one. The land itself will take care of stopping the car as needed. After all, the only other traffic on the plains of Africa likely has four legs, not two.

Even if you couldn't care less about cars, the Experience Drive is a lot of fun. Afterwards, you just might decide that you don't really need a Land Rover in your suburban lifestyle!

Note: *The Heritage Motor Centre, also located in Coventry, is well worth a stop, too. Even non-car aficionados will enjoy the iconic vehicles on display. British car designers "owned" sexy sportscars in the 1960s, many of them built right nearby. You'll find a couple of James Bond Aston Martins as well as a movie space vehicle or two. Of course, everything is beautifully painted, polished, and gleaming.*

Look for the heavily decorated car that completed the very first Pan-American highway journey. You'll learn that the explorers had to spend two months literally hacking their way through the Venezuelan jungle en route!

MEET THE BEATLES PRIVATE TOUR

For many people, the city of Liverpool means one thing: The Beatles. No matter whether you heard them for the first time in the '60s or the '90s or 2020, the four lads' story starts in Liverpool. It's easy to hop a train from London for the two-hour journey northwest to visit this industrial city and discover the roots of the world's most famous rock n' roll group.

Although Liverpool fell on hard times after its heyday as a shipping behemoth, you'll still find many grand buildings reflecting the wealth that all that maritime traffic generated, once upon a time. And if you wonder WHY Liverpool for the Beatles, think about lots of British sailors calling at American ports in the 1950s and returning home to Liverpool with Elvis Presley records in their duffle bags.

Strangely, Liverpool took a long time to acknowledge the fame that the Beatles brought to the city and, more importantly, the role they could play in attracting tourism. Eventually, the city did put up a statue of them and renamed the airport for John Lennon. The Beatles Story Museum, down on the Albert Dock, traces the history of the group. But you can also hire a private guide to focus on the sites and locations central to the Beatles' history.

The childhood homes of John Lennon and Paul McCartney are open for visitors and say much about their origins. You'll see that Paul came from a comfortable middle-class home and John, who grew up primarily with his aunt, from an even more comfortable house. Your guide will note the small plaque that John gave to his aunt, who did not predict success from all that guitar playing. 'Nuff said.

Interestingly, when you see the homes (from the outside) of George and Ringo, you'll see that their young lives were very humble indeed. For all four of them, the transition from middle-class Liverpool to darlings of the world in just a few short years must have been mind-boggling.

Your guide can show you the sign on Penny Lane, as well as the roundabout where "the pretty nurse is selling poppies from a tray." Perhaps you're not aware that poppies are sold in England as a remembrance of the horrors of World War I.

Afterwards, you'll pay a visit to Strawberry Field, the grounds of an old manor home where John Lennon, who lived nearby, played as a child. After falling into disrepair for many years, in 2019, Strawberry Field was opened to the public for the first time, with an exhibition on its history, a cafe, and a shop.

Of course, a stop at St. Peter's Church is a must. Here, you can visit the churchyard where Paul and John first met as teenagers. John's band, the Quarrymen, were booked to play at an outdoor party and John's friend, George Harrison, brought Paul McCartney along as a guest. Be sure to wander a bit in the church graveyard where you'll find the gravestone of Eleanor Rigby.

The Cavern Club, famous as the site of some of the Beatles' first gigs, was eventually torn down, but has been recreated faithfully in downtown Liverpool. It's a simple place; the tiny stage is a raised platform.

Be sure to ask your guide for an extra hour to visit the Casbah Coffee Club. The Casbah occupied a small building attached to the home of Pete Best's mother, Mona. (Of course, you'll remember that Pete Best served as the band's original drummer, replaced by Ringo, on producer George Martin's instructions.) As teenagers, the boys hung out there, decorated the ceiling, and played some early gigs. There are photos to enjoy.

If the Beatles have meant something to you in your own life, pay a few dollars to hire a private guide. It's a great use of money.

TREBUCHET LAUNCH

Once upon a time, a good and noble king lived in a castle with his queen, his three sons, his three daughters, and a legion of the strongest, bravest knights in all of England. He was a fair man who tried to rule his subjects well. However, outside the castle walls, bad men wanted to take over his kingdom, steal his queen, and kill all his children. The king had to defend his castle with strong walls, a moat, a drawbridge, and a portcullis.

Sometimes he had to teach the other kings a lesson: not to attack him. His wisest advisors told him that across the water in France, a new weapon could breach the walls of castles. This modern version of a Roman catapult was called a trebuchet (*tray-boo-shay*). The trebuchet caught on, and soon all the kings had to buy or build a trebuchet to use in their own wars. After many years, castles and trebuchets fell into disuse and were lost to the dusty pages of history.

Centuries later, a cable TV channel decided to make a documentary about old weapons and built a trebuchet to use in the show. They dug out the old history books and they studied the designs, and they built a giant trebuchet. But when they tested it out and tried to launch an enormous stone, they discovered that just building the trebuchet wasn't enough.

They had to practice and practice and adjust the tension and the ropes and the weights so that the projectile would launch in the right direction for the right distance with the right force. Finally, they got the trebuchet to work. Note: *this first modern trebuchet lives at Urquhart Castle in the Scottish Highlands, and the cable TV show was on the History Channel.* Soon, other castle-keepers in England realized that visitors would really enjoy watching a trebuchet in action.

Warwick Castle, near Stratford-upon-Avon, decided to get a trebuchet. Warwick Castle remains the best-preserved castle in all of England, and it looks just like a castle should. A luscious green sward sits in front of it. The castle has towers. It retains intact battlements. (You can walk on them, if you wish.) Ghosts like it. In short, if you're going to visit a castle, choose this one.

The current castle curators have enhanced the medieval experience in numerous ways. In the summer months, Warwick Castle offers themed overnight stays (ghosts invited), jousting tournaments, falconry demonstrations, and other medieval pursuits.

AND...their very large, very impressive trebuchet works. As the largest working trebuchet anywhere, it weighs more than two tons. Twice a day, from April to November, the staff readies the device, loads it up with a projectile and launches it. For a while, they were even offering a flaming projectile launch at night (very dramatic!), but an incident that resulted in a nearby boathouse burning down put an end to that. You'll have to settle for your standard big rock being hurled into space.

What exactly IS a trebuchet? The medieval trebuchet was a "counterweight" trebuchet, as opposed to other varieties. It used a very long arm and a lever to launch a large projectile such as a big rock or a boulder. Typically made from wood, reinforced with metal, leather, rope, or other materials, trebuchets towered thirty feet high or more. Although they sometimes sat on wheels, their bulk and weight made them relatively immobile. A trebuchet crew usually assembled one at the site of a siege outside an enemy castle.

How did it work? In a trebuchet, a long beam was attached by an axle to the frame and base, so that the beam could rotate through a wide arc of more than 180°. The projectile sat in a sling, attached to the long end of a beam. At the short end was a box, usually filled with rocks. On command, the trebuchet team would haul on ropes to lift the heavy box of rocks into the air. When the team released the ropes, the box dropped, and gravity propelled the projectile in the opposite direction. Since it usually took about thirty minutes to load the box of rocks, the trebuchet was not designed for a fast moving battle.

Interestingly, trebuchet users could launch many different things: debris, rotting carcasses, or a flaming object. The rotting carcass sounds a lot like *Monty Python and the Holy Grail*!

If this all sounds intriguing, schedule a stop at Warwick Castle during the trebuchet season. Who doesn't love a great projectile?

FRANCE

AIX-EN-PROVENCE

NIMES

PARIS

OUTDOOR ART WALK AT CHÂTEAU LA COSTE

The charming university town of Aix-en-Provence lies about thirty miles north of Marseille, in southern France. Great food and wine, lovely towns, and an ancient culture have always defined Provence, happily reflected in this small and vibrant city. It's a great stop for travelers doing a river cruise through Provence or those traveling from Avignon over to the French Riviera. And just ten miles outside of town lies Château La Coste.

Home to lovely historic vineyards reimagined and updated for today's world, Château La Coste combines a small all-suite hotel, a great restaurant and wine shop, and a wonderful outdoor art walk. The estate covers more than six hundred acres which provides plenty of room for both the all-important vines and the wonderful artworks and architecture installed.

A small building houses the ticket shop where a giant metallic spider in a tranquil reflecting pool waits to greet you. Lest you personally detest spiders, relax: this spider exhibits a maternal air. She is not at all threatening. Sculpted in 2003 by Louise Bourgeois, she is graceful and elegant and she seems to dance in and above the water. She is the friendliest spider you'll ever meet.

Now prepare to have your artistic sensibilities massaged, intrigued, and stimulated by your walk through the art and architecture garden. There is a clearly defined path to follow if you'd like to explore independently. However, not all of the installations are self-explanatory. You should hire a guide to make sure you can suss out the meaning behind the hidden features of the artworks.

Once you leave the main reception area, you'll encounter sculpture and large multi-part structures dotting the landscape and reflecting it back to you. Whether your artistic tastes run to LeRoy Neiman or Pablo Picasso, you'll find something intriguing along the way. And most of it is big. Really big. As you wander along, the beautiful vineyard land itself merges with the art installations offering you, the visitor, a constantly changing vista.

Your guide can show you which pieces are interactive. That large metallic sphere, rather UFO-ish in shape, seems stationary. It's not. Push it. The meditation bell? Ring it. The silver room? Walk in. The labyrinth with 24,00 bricks? Dare to enter.

You can probably pick out the Alexander Calder work, but you'll be surprised by some of the other contributing artists: Frank Gehry, Paul Matisse, Sean Scully, Richard Serra, Michael Stipe (yes, THAT Michael Stipe), Ai Weiwei. How about a railcar by Bob Dylan? You'll find it here. Want to reflect on negative curvature and infinity? Hiroshi Sugimoto created it for you.

Fans of architecture should spend a few moments at Four Cubes, which focuses on our environment. The artist also built a small and very un-chapel-like Chapel that integrates outside and inside.

Allow time to stop and contemplate along the way while you savor the tranquil views of the vineyards and rural landscape. You'll probably need to allot about two hours to follow the main path on its circuit.

After your walk (or instead of it, depending on your preferences), you might be a tad hungry or parched. No problem: you can relax at a variety of watering holes. An informal outdoor café is perfect for warm weather, while serious gastronomy resides in a more formal restaurant.

The Château and the art walk are open year-round, but winter visitors should dress warmly with water-resistant footwear. Although unlikely, you might encounter a little snow in the vineyards and the more remote sections of the art walk. You will want to be prepared so that you can freely wander off the path to inspect a particular artwork more closely.

KAYAK UNDER THE PONT DU GARD

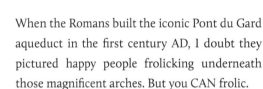

When the Romans built the iconic Pont du Gard aqueduct in the first century AD, I doubt they pictured happy people frolicking underneath those magnificent arches. But you CAN frolic.

The ancient city of Nimes sits in the heart of picturesque Provence. This region of France has always attracted visitors to soak up the beauty of its verdant rolling hills punctuated by simple farmhouses. Here, you can savor classic Provençale cuisine and liberally sample the outstanding local wines. Depending on the season, your eyes may take in enormous fields of lavender or perhaps yellowy-green endless mustard fields. Impressionist artists like Van Gogh and Monet spent time here, creating the memorable images in their paintings.

Nimes harks back to the pre-Roman era, although the Gauls submitted to Roman authority in 121 BCE. The Romans left behind an amphitheater (still in pretty good shape), the beautiful Maison Carrée temple, and even an old tower, the Tour Magne, eventually incorporated into the Roman city wall. But best of all, they built the magnificent aqueduct known as the Pont du Gard, thirty-one kilometers (nineteen miles) outside of town.

The aqueduct carried water all the way to the Tour Magne for eventual distribution throughout the town. Although it hasn't carried water since the sixth century, know that if you visit the Jardins de la Fontaine, on the edge of the city, you can see that the fountain and the canals that flow through it are partly Roman. Those ancient builders knew what they were doing! And once the water stopped flowing (due to a lack of maintenance after the Roman empire collapsed), the lowest level of the aqueduct continued to serve as a toll bridge maintained by the locals.

This magnificent structure stands 160 feet high over the Gardon River. It comprises three tiers of recessed arches, spanning a length of almost 900 feet. Thirty-five arches grace the topmost row, but only six make up the lowest. For the engineering enthusiasts, the numerical details illustrate just how skilled and precise the Roman architects were. Notably, the Romans did not use either mortar or clamps in the construction. Impressive.

Most visitors arrive by car and can see the Pont du Gard from several different vantage points. Taking in the entire structure requires a bit of distance, of course, and most of us will happily marvel at this breathtaking sight.

However, you can paddle right underneath on the calm and clear waters of the Gardon River by kayak during the warmer months (May through September). Several companies offer rentals with the only stipulation being that you can swim twenty-five meters (about twenty-seven yards) and that you're over six years old.

In general, you will put in near the town of Colliers to begin your paddle. The shortest route is about eight kilometers (about six miles) with the passage under the Pont du Gard near the end. At the conclusion of the route, a good kayak company will bring you back by van to the start point. Expect to spend about two hours on the water. You can usually book either a morning or an afternoon trip.

Imagine paddling leisurely along the crystalline waters of the Gardon River amidst the charming landscape of Provence. You have found the proverbial "taking time to smell the roses," far away from your busy life of work, family, errands, responsibilities, and carpooling. Gradually, you can take in the codependence of land and river at sea level. Enjoy each gentle bend of the river's path and the new vistas coming into view as you slowly move along.

Then, suddenly, the enormous and ancient structure of the stately Pont du Gard looms up. It's one thing to see it from above or from a hundred yards away. As you glide beneath it, you experience, in a visceral way, its solidity, its fantastic precision engineering, and its eternal strength. It's 2,000 years old and still standing proud, telling everyone who approaches, "The Romans were here. They invented the Arch. They built this aqueduct/bridge with its beautiful Roman arches." It was meant to last for centuries—and it has.

What a wonderful way to soak up Provence on a warm and sunny day!

PARIS DURING THE WORLD WAR II GERMAN OCCUPATION

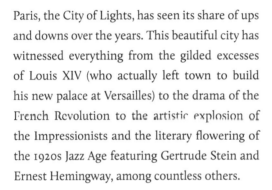

Paris, the City of Lights, has seen its share of ups and downs over the years. This beautiful city has witnessed everything from the gilded excesses of Louis XIV (who actually left town to build his new palace at Versailles) to the drama of the French Revolution to the artistic explosion of the Impressionists and the literary flowering of the 1920s Jazz Age featuring Gertrude Stein and Ernest Hemingway, among countless others.

Sadly, the dark days of the Nazi era led to an occupation in 1940 when the German army marched straight through the iconic Arc de Triomphe and down the Champs-Élysées. Until August of 1944, Paris and its citizens lived as a conquered people. Although countless movies and stories use this time as a historical backdrop, what was it really like for the Parisians? What did "the Resistance" accomplish during that era? How did liberation occur? What are the important sites to know about?

As early as August 1939, the Parisian authorities anticipated a German invasion and began to safeguard the city's artistic treasures. Workmen started taking down the stained-glass windows of Sainte-Chapelle. Curators at the Louvre began cataloging and packing the major works of art into crates labeled only with numbers to disguise their contents. The Winged Victory of Samothrace statue carefully traveled down the long stairway on a wooden ramp to be put on a truck for its departure to the countryside. Scenery trucks for the Comédie Française convoyed the treasures of the Louvre to safety in the castles of the Loire Valley.

In June 1940, the German Army came, and life changed dramatically for the city (and the entire country, of course.) The Arc de Triomphe now bore a giant swastika flag.

Adolf Hitler arrived on June twenty-fourth for a rapid tour by car, guided by the German sculptor Arno Breker and architect Albert Speer, both of whom had lived in Paris. Hitler saw the Opera House and viewed the Eiffel Tower from the terrace of the Palais de Chaillot, paid homage at Napoleon's tomb, and visited the artists' quarter of Montmartre.

As the Germans settled in, their government offices were established in the top hotels of the city. Paris assumed a status of an R&R spot for German soldiers who were each promised a free visit to the city. The city clocks now showed German time and the main boulevards sported German street names.

The occupation lasted four long years of increasing misery, including special punishment for the city's Jews, many of whom were rounded up for transport to Auschwitz. Resistance activities continued throughout the period bringing swift and harsh reprisals.

Finally, the day of liberation came in late August of 1944. With assistance from General Patton's 4th Armored Division, the French 2nd Armored Division of General Leclerc headed to Paris to reclaim the city. German General von Choltitz formally surrendered at the Montparnasse train station. Although an unrepentant Nazi believer, he defied Hitler's order to destroy the city and its monuments.

The descendants of those who lived through the occupation honor those memories to this day. A private guided tour can show you the most important sites, replete with the stories that give meaning to monuments and buildings.

If you're touring independently, start at the Arc de Triomphe where a plaque commemorates the stirring words of General de Gaulle as he rallied his countrymen to keep faith through the coming ordeal.

Heading down the Champs-Élysées, a walk through the Place de la Concorde will take you past the five-star Hotel Crillon, which served as Nazi headquarters. Nearby you can visit the site where the first Resistance newspaper, *Pantagruel*, established itself. Continue to the Place Vendôme, home of the five-star Ritz hotel, which saw both Nazis and Resistance members circling in and out as they went about their business.

Of course, the story of the Jews of Paris deserves special attention and the Marais district hosts several memorials to the hardships they faced. In addition, the Île de la Cité in the middle of the Seine River holds a poignant monument to the 200,000 French Jews who faced deportation.

Plan to end your tour at the Prefecture of Police, near the elegant Hotel de Ville, to focus on the liberation of the city in August of 1944. Be sure to have done your research in advance so that you understand the roles that these monuments and buildings played during this momentous period.

It's likely that the hotel you sleep in or the café where you sip your aperitif bears a tale worth knowing. It takes only a question or two to the right person to bring forth the story.

COCKTAILS ON THE SEINE RIVER

Paris draws visitors from all over the world to savor its cultural riches. From the stark metal superstructure of the Eiffel Tower to the smaller-than-expected *Mona Lisa* in the Louvre to the elegant Tuileries Gardens to the dramatic Notre-Dame cathedral, Paris boasts some of the most iconic sights on our planet, all grouped together in one glorious confection of broad boulevards, cobbled streets, formal public squares, churches, gardens, quirky shops, and bookstores.

On every corner, cafes and bistros invite you to linger over a coffee or a glass of wine while you channel your favorite historical and literary figures. Leonardo da Vinci. The Hunchback of Notre-Dame. Poor Marie Antoinette who lost her head. The Three Musketeers. Napoleon. Ernest Hemingway and Gertrude Stein. Picasso. Monet. De Gaulle. Call forth your favorites for a little "sip and sigh."

Like many historic cities, Paris got its start because of a river, the Seine. In fact, the first settlers camped on the Île de la Cité, in the middle of the river. It was easier to defend for obvious reasons. Here, you'll find some of the oldest buildings in the city, now dwarfed by Notre-Dame Cathedral recovering after the disastrous fire of 2019.

The Seine actually starts about 225 miles southwest of Paris in Dijon, Burgundy, flowing 485 miles north and west through the heart of Paris before emptying into the English Channel. Although it is a long and strong river, within the city limits stone embankments on either side control and direct it, making for long quays along which Parisians stroll, eat, sip wine, make love, and occasionally dance. And they often buy books from bookstalls that have lined the river for several hundred years.

All of this life on the banks of the Seine makes for a very pleasant ride on the river. Yes, you can hop on the famous Bateaux Mouches (literally "fly boats") or the Navettes for a one-hour tour. That's a well-known option. You can also enjoy lunch or dinner on board if you wish, but the main attraction is the city itself, seen from the water.

Amp it up a notch and hire a private motorboat for a sunset sail through the heart of the city. Choose a craft small enough for two or big enough for a party of twelve. And if you're thinking "we need a bigger boat," invite twenty-five of your most intimate friends along. No problem.

The lovely teak wood of a classic Venetian-style yacht is inherently inviting. The cruise can be a lovely hour and a half for cocktails, canapés, and champagne at sunset or a three-hour extravaganza of cocktails, champagne, and a four-course dinner.

Imagine leisurely putt-putting along this fabled waterway with a glass of bubbly in hand, surrounded by one of the most beautiful cities in the world. The flying buttresses of Notre-Dame appear magically in front of you. You'll circle the island for an up close and strikingly beautiful view of this famous cathedral. West of Notre-Dame, your friendly captain will point out the iconic sights of the Right Bank: the former Palais Royale (now the Louvre Museum), the lovely Tuileries Gardens, the Place de la Concorde and, eventually, the Eiffel Tower.

Do you know that in the evening, every hour on the hour, the Eiffel Tower features a light display with a sparkling orb at the very top? It's a magical sight, even better from the river with an unobstructed view!

You'll float gently under the bridges, learning the characteristics and history of each one. And they all tell their own stories, of course. One is named for a Russian czar. Another is the "love lock" bridge. The oldest of them all is the Pont Neuf, the first one to connect the major roads of the city back in the 1500s. There are actually thirty-seven bridges in Paris, and the ones in the city center are yours for the viewing from below.

The Seine is a busy waterway during the day, helping fuel the commerce of the city. However, as the workday subsides, so does the boat traffic, making for a peaceful evening sojourn on the water.

A private boat on the Seine at sunset is about as romantic an experience as you can imagine. It would certainly provide an exquisite setting for a marriage proposal...a family celebration of a fortieth wedding anniversary...or a fiftieth birthday celebration with your college friends. The possibilities are endless!

GERMANY

FRIEDRICHSHAFEN
BERLIN
POTSDAM

ZEPPELIN FLIGHT OVER LAKE CONSTANCE

Are you one of those people fascinated by blimps and zeppelins, those giant airborne cucumbers that seem to float effortlessly through the sky? While blimp experiences are hard to come by (think charity giveaways or celebrity promotions), a zeppelin experience is do-able. You just need to get yourself to southern Germany and the Lake Constance (Bodensee) region.

Zeppelins owe their origins to a German engineer named...wait for it...Ferdinand von Zeppelin, back in 1893. Unlike the soft-sided blimps made famous by Goodyear in the US, a zeppelin uses a rigid skeleton and achieves lift from hydrogen gas. Once heralded for elegant, long-distance, and transatlantic flights, zeppelins fell out of favor after the Hindenburg disaster and World War II. However, modern zeppelins still offer short flight-seeing excursions in the area around Lake Constance and Munich.

This gorgeous region in southern Germany comprises small medieval villages, castles, and palaces on Lake Constance, along with colorful islands and the foothills of the Alps. Floating along at about three hundred yards above the earth (roughly the height of the Eiffel Tower), a zeppelin allows you a perfect position to gaze down, gaze out, and gaze up at one of the most enchanting regions of Germany. Your leisurely float proceeds at about thirty miles per hour, giving you lots of time to watch as your airship's shadow gracefully crosses over the sailboats on the lake below. Or perhaps you'll channel a medieval experience as you look down upon a picturesque walled village from the past.

Zeppelins are a marvel of construction and aficionados can spend time in the hangar before, after, or instead of a flight. A hangar tour can explain the history and the modern technology of zeppelins. Plus, while you're there, just watching some take offs and landings is a lot of fun.

We're all so used to the normality of a standard airplane flight with its taxi and acceleration down a runway, a steep climb-out, the flight at cruising altitude and then the corresponding descent, eventual wheeled landing, and rapid deceleration on another runway. The zeppelin doesn't do any of those things and still gets itself into the air, which tends to grab our attention when we see it in action.

A zeppelin weighs about 2,400 pounds, marrying its relatively light weight to high stability. It consists of twelve segments of triangular carbon fiber crossbeams connected to three longerons (a load-bearing component) made from welded aluminum. Aramid (synthetic fiber) ropes brace the whole structure and give it extra rigidity. All the major components, like the cabin, the fins, and the engines, are mounted right on the zeppelin, allowing for enhanced maneuvering ability.

A small cabin attached to the underside of the air chamber allows for a group of up to fourteen passengers to ride along with the pilot and copilot. Naturally, big picture windows and comfortable seats offer you great bird's-eye views. You can charter the zeppelin for a private event or celebration if you wish, although be prepared to dig into your pocket pretty deeply for this one.

Flightseeing excursions last from a half hour to 120 minutes, depending on the exact route chosen. You can select everything from a forty-five-minute flight over the city of Munich to a viewing of the dramatic Rhine Falls at Schaffhausen to an itinerary over Lindau and Bregenz, including the famous waterside theater. Your view from the heavens is going to be pretty great, no matter what you choose.

Afterwards, drop in the nearby garden paradise of Mainau Island for a treat for your senses. Over one hundred acres is home to impressive gardens including a Rhododendron Slope, Italian Rose Garden, Dahlia Garden, and Hydrangea Path.

PRIVATE TRAINCAR TRAVEL

Channel your inner Rockefeller and claim your private rail car for a special outing on the German rail system. If the industrial robber barons could commandeer the tracks for their own comfort, so can you. Imagine leisurely traversing a landscape without the need to consult the GPS or stop for a snack along the way. All of your needs for comfort, food, and drink will be met seamlessly on board.

First things first: design a route for your journey, knowing that if the rail station exists within Germany, you can use it for arrival or departure. The only real requirement is that everyone arrives and departs at the same time, using the same stations. In other words, you cannot stop and "pick up" someone en route. All passengers need to accompany you from beginning to end. Aside from that, you can set your own route, choosing places that have special meaning just for you.

This private journey uses a luxurious dome-car with large picture windows for viewing the rural landscape as you relax with your traveling companions. Perhaps you'll choose the southern landscape, taking in the gorgeous Bavarian Alps.

Or skirt lovely Lake Constance and Bregenz? The Black Forest near the Rhine? Or traverse the charming Harz mountains between Hamburg and Berlin? So many possibilities.

You can choose up to twenty of your most intimate (and lucky) friends to share the occasion. As part of your special private car, a lounge in the back of the train or the bar in the front can serve as a private retreat for a special moment. Marriage proposal? Actually, you might want a friend with a camera on hand for that one.

Take it up a notch and add a private two-star Michelin chef to your event. Any train aficionado knows the magic of combining delicious cuisine and well-chosen wine pairings with a beautiful landscape slipping by big picture windows. The experience is bound to evoke all kinds of images of romance, intrigue, and adventure. Perhaps Cary Grant will walk right through the train to join you for dinner!

GRAFFITI TOUR OF BERLIN

Berlin is a city of many, many layers. It stands for the source of all evil in hundreds of books and movies about World War II. It stands as a visible line of tension in countless novels and books about the Cold War. It boasts an island in the city center with no less than five art museums on it. What is clear is that Berlin is more than just those twelve awful years in the 1930s and '40s.

Berlin lives in flux. Perhaps for that reason, artists of all media have often gravitated to the city, making for a vibrant art scene. As sections of the city evolve, particularly in the old Eastern half, denizens of cafés and art galleries now live side by side with free spirits who occupy rundown and inexpensive housing. Think Greenwich Village in the 1950s. Political protest, free expression, and artistic whimsy are on public display, particularly in Kreuzberg and Friedrichshain.

Your first stop should be the still-standing portion of the Berlin Wall where you'll find portrayals of mostly political imagery. Although artists originally painted their works *ad hoc* starting in 1990 when the wall came down, over time the city invited artists from all over the world to make their statements on this long section of the preserved wall.

Some of the most famous images include *Fraternal Kiss* (showing former USSR leader Brezhnev and East German leader Honecker in each other's arms) and *Trabant Breaking Through the Wall*. A Trabant was the people's car of the old East Germany.

You'll also want to wander around Kreuzberg and Friedrichshain. These are hip, new areas in transition where artists have taken any available space to express themselves. Some of the images are recognizable; others are more abstract. Coffee bars and small shops dot the labyrinthine streets, and any available wall serves as a "canvas" for an artist or two.

Because the art is widely dispersed over these differing sections of the city, hiring a guide (a local artist) to show you the highlights makes a lot of sense. Your guide can direct you to the most impressive pieces, after which you can meet with local practitioners who can show you some of their techniques in a workshop.

After feeding your cultural senses for several hours, you might want to stop at an open-air food bazaar to mix with the locals and satisfy your hunger. Of course, you should include a beer for the most authentic experience.

THE BRIDGE OF SPIES

Most visitors to Berlin spend two or three days touring the city with its western and eastern halves, the Dom (Cathedral), Museum Island, and Cold War relics like Checkpoint Charlie. But a simple thirty-minute trip by local train to Potsdam highlights some of the most dramatic Cold War history ever, encapsulated in the Bridge of Spies.

At the Potsdam train station, buy a ticket for the hop on, hop off bus tour, which includes stops at several fine palaces and gardens from the age of Frederick the Great. On board, you'll hear some good stories of royal gossip, intrigue, and even some dog history, preparing you to wander around the extensive royal grounds. Although not open to the public, the little Sans-Souci palace hosted Truman, Churchill, and Stalin in the closing days of World War II while they discussed the shape of a new Europe.

After you've had your fill of monarchs and glitz, hop back on the bus and have your camera ready for the Glienicke Bridge, host to numerous spy exchanges during the Cold War. Although not the focus of the tour, the bus will drive over the bridge and back, making for a great photo op.

Yes, this is the bridge where Tom Hanks waited to trade Soviet spy Rudolf Abel for the downed U-2 pilot Gary Powers in the film *Bridge of Spies*. It's a modest little structure spanning Lake Wannsee. Although not very high and not very long, Glienicke Bridge has played an outsized role in history. Why?

When the Soviet Union soldiers arrived in Germany and eventually Berlin at the end of World War II, they avenged Hitler's invasion of their homeland in numerous, unsavory ways. The Soviet government didn't leave until the fall of the Berlin Wall in 1989.

As World War II ended, an unexploded shell severely damaged the bridge. The East German government rebuilt it in 1949, renaming it the Unity Bridge and leaving it under the sway of the Soviet Union for decades. Because the bridge connected the border of West Germany and East Germany, it also served as a checkpoint between Cold War opponents. The East German government declared it off limits to West Germans in 1952 and to East Germans in 1961 when they constructed the Berlin Wall. Its very location eventually made it convenient for intelligence agencies to trade spies and the occasional political prisoner between East and West.

After the Russians declared the land on the East German side of the bridge off limits to Germans, the KGB took over the entire area. In fact, KGB headquarters for all Eastern Europe relocated here. In the barracks-like buildings adjacent to the bridge, prisoners waited for their exchange. For more than forty years after the end of that terrible war, Germans did not control this piece of their own territory. They called it "The Forbidden City."

After Gary Powers was shot down from his U-2 flight in 1960, the Soviet Union staged a show trial which ended in his conviction and imprisonment. Two years later, lawyer James Donovan successfully negotiated a prisoner exchange for Soviet spy Rudolf Abel, setting the stage for the dramatic trade. Notably, the Russians did not want to exchange the two men at Checkpoint Charlie in Berlin where they felt that the Americans would receive a lot of favorable publicity. Glienicke Bridge, off limits to just about everyone, was perfect.

On February 12, 1962, handlers brought the two men to separate sides of the Glienicke Bridge. As the spies waited, negotiators talked in the center of the bridge where a severe white line and "no man's land" divided East from West. Finally, Powers and Abel were waved forward and crossed the border at the same moment at 8:52 am. Imagine the drama as each man moved forward, everyone wondering if someone would get a shot in the back and what would happen then. But the exchange occurred without incident, and both sides retreated to their safe havens.

Glienecke Bridge witnessed other notable exchanges. On June 12, 1985, the Soviet Union swapped twenty-three American agents held in Eastern Europe for Polish agent Marian Zacharski and another three Soviet agents over the bridge. On February 11, 1986, the Soviet human rights campaigner Anatoly Shcharansky (now known as Natan Sharansky) and three Western agents traded places with Karl Koecher and four other Eastern agents on the bridge.

Although real events carry enough drama themselves, the Bridge has also served as a location in numerous spy novels, including John le Carré's trilogy *Smiley's People* and Len Deighton's *Funeral in Berlin*.

To cap your daytrip, when you're back in Berlin, walk by the Russian Embassy on Unter den Linden and look for the Soviet Hammer and Sickle, embedded in the frieze of the facade. Yup. Still there.

ICELAND

REYKJAVIK

FOOD AND FUN FESTIVAL ICELAND

Iceland is a VERY short flight from either Europe or the United States. In fact, it takes less time to fly from New York to Reykjavik than it does to California. That means that a fun long weekend is yours for the asking. In four-and-a-half short hours from New York, Boston, or a number of other cities, you can hop across the Atlantic to this unique little Scandinavian island.

It's true that the high season for tourism occurs in the summer months when temperatures warm and much of this amazing country turns from white to green. But Iceland is a perfectly viable winter getaway, too—especially if you plan for the Food and Fun Festival in Reykjavik, held annually in late February or early March since 2002.

Too cold? Not really. Anyone who knows and loves New England or the Midwest will find that a blustery New York January day feels colder than Reykjavik in February. For sure, you need to bring your winter gear and sweaters, but the weather does not inhibit the fun—or your dining pleasure.

During the festival, Reykjavik invites chefs from both sides of the Atlantic to a gastronomical competition for five days. Each chef takes over a specific restaurant and creates his or her own four-course menu. During the Food and Fun Festival, each restaurant serves only that chef's creations each day. You'll enjoy a set menu featuring appetizers, main entrée, second entrée, and dessert. The restaurants are not required to participate in the competition, but most of the best ones do.

Each course serves as a separate entry in the competition and can incorporate only local components for the centerpieces of their dishes. The chefs concentrate on freshness and variety in the Icelandic ingredients such as fish, free range and unique lamb, and organic dairy products. The clean surroundings and sustainable agriculture of this natural wonderland are on full display during the competition. And the results are delicious.

To enhance the culinary creations and experiences, each chef and restaurant offers suggested wine pairings for the meal. Of course, the wine pairings are optional, and you can choose whether to simply enjoy dining or savor a full wining and dining experience.

As a visitor, you can either follow a particular chef or pick a specific restaurant for each night that you are there. Reservations are required since these establishments are not very big. Nothing in Iceland is very big (except for Thingvellir, but that's a different story.) Some of the restaurants inhabit former houses with different rooms; others are in small buildings. Without a reservation, you may not get to dine where or when you wish.

The festival has grown in popularity since its founding and some chefs apply but do not make the cut due to a lack of available restaurants. Of course, we, the happy diners, reap the gastronomic rewards of all this friendly competition.

If you fear that visiting this northern country in winter will mean perpetual darkness, fear not. Each month in Iceland, sunlight increases and decreases by three hours. That means that a visitor in December loses a lot of touring time while the summer visitor enjoys the land of the midnight sun. And for a March visit? You're almost at the equinox with equal day and night. Thus, for lots of reasons, a long weekend in Iceland in March makes for a perfect getaway.

Put your passport in your bag, your biodegradable straw in your pocket, and your napkin in your lap. What a great way to sprint toward the finish line of winter's end and the start of spring!

IRELAND

DROMOLAND
DUBLIN
KILLARNEY
SKELLIG MICHAEL

WALK WITH A FALCON

The small country of Ireland boasts lively cities like Dublin and Belfast, gorgeous lakes, dramatic mountains, famous sites like the Ring of Kerry and Giant's Causeway, and wild regions like the Dingle Peninsula. Ireland is also well known for its love of traditions like thoroughbred horse racing and breeding. Interestingly, in recent years, a number of sites have arisen to allow visitors to get up close and personal with another one of Ireland's traditions: falconry.

Falconry has a long and storied history, dating back possibly as far as 2,000 BCE in the steppes of Mongolia. In Ireland, as early as the twelfth century, writers referred to hunting hawks. Over the years, Ireland acquired a reputation for providing excellent quality hawks. Hawk breeders could make a decent living and Kilkenny Castle's fourteenth century documents list different kinds of hawks that could be used to pay rent.

Hawks originally aided in hunting for food, of course. However, the invention of gunpowder made hawks less useful in obtaining food, and the process of hunting with hawks migrated to a leisure pastime, acquiring the moniker "the Sport of Kings."

Using a hawk for hunting requires the falcon to accept a human as a hunting partner. Once accustomed to a human presence, the falcon learns to take food from the falconer's glove. Next, the master trains the bird to step on the heavy leather glove for a food treat and eventually to fly onto the glove to get the reward. (The glove protects a human arm and hand from the seriously sharp and strong talons of the hawks.) Because hawks don't really need humans as a food source, falconry trainers generally don't release the birds into areas with plentiful prey. The raptors live about fifteen years on average and stay with their "owners" for food and companionship.

If you would like to see just what a hawk or a falcon can really do, stop in at a raptor center. Ireland offers numerous opportunities throughout the countryside. Be sure to choose a program that allows you to accompany a falconer and his bird on a "walk/flyby" so that the bird can really demonstrate his/her talents.

Your falcon friend undoubtedly lives under the careful tutelage of his master, owner of the leather glove, the hood, and the other necessary accoutrements of falconry. On a walk in the country and through a wooded area, your friendly falcon will periodically fly on and off the master's glove while you walk and learn about falcons and falconry. Master and bird share an amazing bond.

You can watch while the falcon takes some food from his master while on the glove and then flies off into a nearby tree. When his master holds up a speck of something that the falcon likes, that bird will reappear in the blink of an eye. With their hawk-eye vision, these birds can see objects from more than a mile away. A peregrine falcon, the fastest of all raptors, displays a dive speed of about 180 miles per hour and a third eyelid that closes during a dive to protect the eyes.

Ideally, the falconry master will invite you to put on the leather glove and allow the falcon to alight there. Watching a hunting bird fly toward you at a high speed does require some confidence that this is going to turn out okay for both bird and human. You'll be able to feel his heavy, sharp talons through the leather, but a well-trained bird will perch there quite sedately, with excellent manners.

You may experience the following pattern: New human in a glove. Falcon master places a piece of meat in sight of a bird that is out of sight, up in a tree. Falcon flies and lands on the glove. A picture is taken.

And now for some fun: perhaps your falcon will retreat up into a tree, out of sight, out of YOUR sight that is. That bird can see you QUITE clearly. Perhaps your falcon master will distract you with a speech about falcon sleeping habits and while you're paying attention, toss a piece of meat casually into the air. Watch that falcon dive at 180 miles per hour out of nowhere and snatch that piece of meat in mid-air. It is a breathtaking moment.

Countless local programs introduce children to animals, including large reptiles and even raptors. But watching a raptor sit sedately on a glove at a small library cannot compare to watching a falcon dive and hunt in the woods.

Falconry can be found in various locations around Ireland. However, not all raptor centers allow for individual interaction with the birds while they go out for exercise. Choose carefully to make sure that your experience respects the bird's health and well-being.

KILMAINHAM GAOL

When you plan your visit to Dublin, you'll undoubtedly include stops to see the richly decorated, medieval Book of Kells at Trinity College, the wonderful and inventive Guinness Brewery museum, a walk along Grafton Street, and perhaps an evening in Temple Bar to sample trendy restaurants and pubs. However, if you want to understand how Ireland came to be Ireland, schedule a visit to Kilmainham Gaol, easily accessible from the hop-on-hop-off bus route.

A gaol? Ghoulish? Macabre? Like Alcatraz in San Francisco? No, Kilmainham Gaol is none of those things. While indeed many sad and miserable things happened there during its existence, the gaol tells a remarkable story.

Dating back to 1796, Kilmainham Gaol housed both men and women (and even children) as criminals and political prisoners. Although eventually decommissioned in 1924, its use as a place of punishment for political prisoners in the first part of the twentieth century reflects the tumultuous formation of the modern Irish state.

Most of us know that Ireland existed as an unhappy British colony for many, many years.

The Potato Famine of the 1860s that sent so many starving Irish people to other countries, including the United States, punctuates its sad history.

In the first part of the 1900s, an Easter uprising in Dublin signaled a new commitment by locals to throwing off British rule at last. It was a bloody Sunday, and the rebellion failed. The British soldiers violently repressed the movement, throwing many of the rebels arrested into Kilmainham Gaol.

The British government administered punishment harshly before executing most (but not all) of the leaders of the uprising by firing squad in the yard. Your tour will show you not only the dark and damp cells, but also the yard and the wall before which the unlucky prisoners lined up before their deaths.

Notably, one of the rebellion leaders, Éamon de Valera, was NOT executed. He happened to have an American mother and the British government did not want to risk alienating Woodrow Wilson during World War I. They wanted the US to enter the war on the British side and felt that executing de Valera might preclude that possibility. Thus, de Valera escaped the firing squad.

A few short years later, in the 1920s, Ireland struggled between opposing Irish patriots. Some favored the new Irish Free State, negotiated as a Treaty with England; others disliked the treaty that kept Ireland in the British Commonwealth and required swearing allegiance to the British King. The conflict was deadly and violent, and it raged for several years.

As the pro-treaty patriots gained power and sought to consolidate it, they arrested anti-treaty patriots and threw them into Kilmainham Gaol (again). Now, some of their former co-prisoners served as their guards. Éamon de Valera found himself back at Kilmainham, as a prisoner again. His fortunes continued to swing in subsequent years and eventually he served as president of a new Ireland.

Meanwhile, after the Gaol was decommissioned, it fell into great disrepair until a grassroots movement arose in the 1950s to preserve and restore it as a place central to Ireland's history. Many people devoted their free labor to the restoration, including several former prisoners. They, too, wanted to commemorate the suffering that occurred there, lest it vanish in the dusk of time. When the restoration was complete, an aged Éamon de Valera presided over the reopening of Kilmainham Gaol as a museum.

Today, Kilmainham Gaol tells its story to visitors, representing an important facet of Irish history. Be sure to get the audio guide, which is excellent and adds much more to this living history. And if you've never heard of Éamon de Valera, by the time you leave, you'll understand the special role that he played in the story of modern Ireland.

GAP OF DUNLOE

The small country of Ireland is a land of contrasts. In the east, you'll find Dublin and Belfast. In the west country, big open spaces dominate, and it is here that you'll find the Lake District of County Kerry. As the name suggests, this area in the southwest boasts numerous lakes, set off by green hills, stone walls, and big vistas. The small town of Killarney sits at its center, serving as an easy location from which you can explore the famed Ring of Kerry, a stunningly beautiful road that encircles a small peninsula. Yes, driving the Ring of Kerry is a wonderful outing, but you, my friend, are going to do something different than the busloads of tourists typically do.

Near Killarney, you'll also find the Gap of Dunloe, a small mountain pass that allows you to transit from the Purple Mountain Group in the east to MacGillycuddy's Reeks in the west, ending at a series of small lakes. "Doing" the Gap of Dunloe makes for a great day out, whether you want a full hike with lots of exercise or a gentler version: your choice.

Get yourself to little Kate Kearney's Cottage, west of Killarney. Grab a few provisions and lace up your sneakers before you set off along the gentle incline, up through the Gap.

As you meander along the rocky dirt road, small hills, classic Irish stone walls, and a small stream punctuate the rocky landscape. You may need to accommodate a few cyclists or jaunting carts as they trot gently beside you. A jaunting cart is a small horse and trap with a driver and room for three or four passengers. You may even occasionally see a sturdy and determined car, but not many of those drivers want to risk their tires here.

This evocative six-mile walk leads steadily upward with plenty of time to stop and take in the scenery. Perhaps you'll rest beside the stream (the Loe River) or partake of a little sustenance or libation along the way. If you make a wish at the Wishing Bridge, chances are it will come true.

After you crest the hill, the descent takes you slowly down past simple houses to a small lakeside pub (Lord Brandon's cottage) where you can refresh yourself after the hike. Sooner or later, a small boat will stop and pick up any waiting passengers for a small fee.

Your chatty Irish pilot will ferry you back to Killarney through a series of connected serene lakes, telling tall tales along the way. The more you chat, the better the stories. Smiles are guaranteed for all but the stoniest countenances.

Soon enough, he will deposit you at the small boat dock in Killarney. If you ask him exactly how long the walk through the Gap actually is, he might answer with a smile and a wink, "Oh, six miles and a bit—where the bit is more than a mile."

If you find the six-mile hike a bit daunting, you can hire one of the jaunting carts at Kate Kearney's cottage. The jaunting cart will carry you to the top of the Gap, giving you the "gentle" version of the outing. You can probably arrange for both the drop off at Kate Kearney's cottage and the return transfer from the pier in Killarney through your hotel concierge.

LUKE SKYWALKER'S LAST HOME

Attention Star Wars aficionados! Once upon a time, in a galaxy far, far away, director George Lucas created a whole world for Luke Skywalker. While it's a tad arduous to visit Tatooine, you can easily stop by Luke's last abode on your next trip to Ireland. A forty-five-minute ferry ride from Portmagee in County Kerry will bring you to the small and rocky island of Skellig Michael, eight miles off the southwest coast. Here, Luke Skywalker sought to punish himself in his final years in a harsh and inhospitable landscape, as seen in *The Force Awakens* and *The Last Jedi*.

There are actually two Skellig islands, Skellig Michael, aka Great Skellig, and Little Skellig. Both islands are well known for their seabird colonies, host to northern gannets and kittiwakes and puffins and peregrine falcons who all find the local environment inviting.

Skellig Michael lent itself perfectly to the needs of George Lucas when he wanted to put Luke Skywalker in a place of self-punishment. The island is rocky and barren and windswept. Not much grows there and most people don't want to live there.

However, in the distant past, the monastic order of St. Fionán decided to establish an outpost on Skellig Michael, and they built a crude monastery there sometime in the sixth century. Due to changing climate conditions, after several hundred years, the monks moved back to the mainland. However, their conical stone dwellings remain. That's what we all see in the Star Wars movies.

The huts are round on the outside and rectangular within. Given the harsh and rainy nature of the environment, the monks constructed huts designed to be watertight—and they still are. Other structures still visible today include a large oratory, the ruins of the church, a graveyard, crosses, and retaining walls.

The monks built three sets of steps to their monastery, affording access during differing weather conditions. Only one set of steps, the south steps, is accessible by the public today. The three flights of stairs start as rock-cut steps and then change to dry stone once they are out of reach of rough seas. As you wind your way up, you'll get dramatic views of the mainland and Little Skellig.

On the way up, you'll encounter one long flight, which leads up to Christ's Saddle, a good place to catch your breath before continuing up to the monastery itself. At the top of the access steps, you'll see a nineteenth century entrance which leads into the Upper Monks' Garden. You'll find the original entrance at the other end of this garden, located at the top of the east steps.

Imagine a life of contemplation and isolation on this remote island in the Atlantic. Supposedly, about twelve ascetic monks spent their days praying in the church, studying, and tending to the gardens. The retaining walls created a small microclimate, suitable for growing plants and vegetables. After the monks returned to the mainland, Skellig Michael became a place of pilgrimage.

In the Star Wars era, movie fans have put Skellig Michael on the map, and you are now required to get a ticket to visit the island. Only 180 people are allowed to visit per day, and they mostly arrive at the same time. Be aware that you will have company as you poke around.

Because you need a boat to get there, anyone inclined to nausea should note that the seas can be rough with high winds. In fact, passage is not guaranteed and is weather-dependent.

Once on the island, you will have about two hours to explore on your own. Guides stationed along various pathways will help you and provide instruction. You do need to stay on the paths as marked because some of the narrow pathways can be dangerous, especially if rain has made the paths slippery. Good hiking shoes are a must; no flip-flops if you want to avoid a sprained ankle.

Also, it's important to note that the current interest in Skellig Michael has not translated into restroom facilities or services of any kind. So "go" before you go.

Some preservationists have cited damage to the island from both filming of the movies and the resulting waves of visitors who want to see the Skywalker environment. Steps leading to the monastery have needed repair, as a result. In addition, there is some dissatisfaction locally that the Star Wars associations have superceded the islands' 1,400-year history. Before the movies' release, hardly anyone went to Skellig Michael. Since then, daytrips have become a source of revenue for local boat owners from Port Magee. And the long view notes that the harsh climate conditions have eroded this little island for thousands of years. You can weigh all of these factors as you decide whether to make your "pilgrimage" or not.

Alternatively, you can see the islands and enjoy the local marine life on a boat tour that circles both islands but does not land on either of them.

ITALY

BOMARZO
CAPRI
RAVELLO
ROME
SABAUDIA
SORRENTO
TIVOLI
VENICE

PARCO DEI MOSTRI
(PARK OF THE MONSTERS)

Italy boasts some justly famous Renaissance gardens. The Villa d'Este, the Villa Lante, the Vatican Gardens, and the Boboli Gardens have all delighted the eye and the senses for hundreds of years. However, one man had a different idea.

About forty-five miles north of Rome on the busy Superstrada, keep your eyes open for the exit to the small town of Bomarzo, famous for its unique and bizarre Parco dei Mostri. As you leave the highway, follow the signs down the dusty, desolate, and deserted road to the park. Have faith because the signs are small, and you may be the only car on this little road. Park and prepare for a very unusual Renaissance garden.

In the sixteenth century, Vicino Orsini hired Pirro Ligorio (the most famous architect of his day) and spent his money to construct a personal monument to unusual ideas. His motivation? There are two theories.

Theory number one: After his wife died, he found solace in building an unusual tribute to her. (Um, if this was my husband's "tribute" to me, I'd lay out some specific instructions instead.)

Theory number two: Orsini was appalled at the enormous sums of money that high-ranking church leaders had spent on their pet projects, personified by the Villa d'Este gardens in Tivoli and the Villa Lante in nearby Bagnaia. In a perversion of the official mission of the church, these men had devoted vast sums and untold labor to vanity projects. Orsini created a garden to proclaim his distaste for the twisted and cynical society he saw around him.

The *mostri* (monsters) consist of giant, grotesque sculptures that portray unsettling and threatening images. You'll meet a sea monster and her offspring. You'll observe Hannibal's elephant catching a Roman legionary. You'll see a monster holding a soldier upside down before his imminent demise. You can stand in the mouth of an enormous and unfriendly looking fish. You can gaze at some anonymous ancient gods with blunt features and strange expressions.

The garden is built on a hillside, and after you've gawked at the bizarre statuary, wander up. Eventually you will come to a small house (*casita*) which deliberately sits askew. You'll bend your head to try to "right" it, but to no avail. Yes, you can go in, and as you wander through it, you'll see crooked walls. You'll stand on floors that are slanting. It's all "off" by design. This was Orsini's ultimate statement, realized in stone for permanence.

After Orsini's death, the garden gradually fell into decline and was largely forgotten. In the twentieth century, some of our more adventurous artists rediscovered it. Yes, Jean Cocteau and Salvador Dali thought it was just great—naturally! In fact, Dali's painting *The Temptation of St. Anthony* was supposedly inspired by the park.

You may or may not want to create a film or paint after your visit, but I'll bet you take home a picture of yourself standing in the mouth of that fish!

For the best contrast, visit the beautiful Villa Lante garden in nearby Bagnaia first to understand why Orsini might have wanted to create his monsters.

FAMOUS NAMES OF CAPRI

This sun-kissed island off the coast of Naples has attracted visitors from afar forever. Everyone from Ulysses to Roman Emperors to Russian revolutionaries to movie stars of today has found a reason to linger here.

Augustus Caesar thought it perfect for his summer vacation. His successor, Tiberius, built a large pleasure palace for his own retirement when he'd had enough of Rome. In truth, there are a lot of seedy rumors about Tiberius in his later days on Capri, but I will leave those nasty details to someone else. Fast forward two-thousand years and you'll find the *glitterati* still seeking its fabled shores.

What's the attraction? Soaring cliffs, drop-dead scenery, warm breezes, sparkling cobalt waters, the fresh aroma of lemons, and a climate that seems to feature eternal sunshine while storms lash the mainland towns all contribute to making Capri a mythical, magical, and appealing place. If you keep your eyes open as you stroll about and learn a little bit of the local history, you will find traces of many famous visitors over the years. Or hire a private guide to focus on who did what and where.

In modern times, starting in the late 1800s, Europeans began to migrate here for a restorative period, sometimes staying for years. The trend continued throughout the 1900s, and the island continues to enchant the world today.

Poets, philosophers, artists, industrialists, aristocratic exiles, and more than one Russian revolutionary have all found solace among the hospitable population, the car-less pathways of Capri town, and the beautiful landscapes on every side. You might recognize the names of the painter Karl Diefenbach, Friedrich Krupp of the German steel fortune, composer Claude Debussy, writers Thomas Mann, Oscar Wilde, Henry James, and Graham Greene, and the Chilean poet Pablo Neruda, to name just a few.

Krupp lived in a suite of rooms at the wonderful Hotel Quisisana in the center of Capri Town. His interest in marine biology kept him there and he eventually bought land for a villa. After the war, his property was converted into the Augustan Gardens, a public park with gorgeous views of the Faraglioni rocks and the bay of Marina Piccola. There is a small hotel adjacent to the park, called Villa Krupp. Although Krupp never lived there himself, the Russian revolutionary writer Maxim Gorky did.

Gorky, already a successful and wealthy writer, joined the Bolshevik Party in Russia in 1905, well before the revolution in 1917. His money helped seed some of the activities of the revolutionaries as they planned their first uprising against the czar in 1905. The next year, traveling with his famous Russian actress lover, Gorky arrived in Naples, eventually moving on to Capri where he parked himself for six years. Imagine the choice he had to make: Moscow fall, winter, and spring bundled up in furs to survive OR....sunny Capri with its cypress trees, mild winters, and sunshine. I think we can all agree he made the right decision.

At first, he ensconced himself in the Hotel Quisisana in the center of Capri Town but soon moved to more "suitable" quarters in the Villa Krupp. One of his visitors was actually Vladimir Lenin, founder of Russian Communism. Should we call Capri the birthplace of the Russian Revolution? Gorky actually started a school to educate the local working class about the joys of Communism, but the laborers and their wives just didn't take to it. In 1913, Gorky went home to Mother Russia.

Fast forward to World War II and the dark days of Fascism during which time Italy allied itself with Germany. In 1943, the Allies launched their invasion of the continent through Italy at Salerno, on the Bay of Naples. Capri Island was a convenient place for Eisenhower to live for several months while the Italian campaign was operating. Villa Punta Tragara at the end of a long but scenic pathway served as his headquarters, and you can find a plaque attesting to his stay on the wall of the Punta Tragara Hotel. During this time, Winston Churchill visited to confer about the situation and adjust their battle strategy.

After the war ended in 1945, Capri began yet another phase of popularity, this time with the international jetset. In fact, a new style of short, cropped pants for women was introduced in 1948 and tagged "Capri pants"—a name still in vogue today. Actresses of that era, including Audrey Hepburn, Marilyn Monroe, and Brigitte Bardot, all sported the snug fitting style.

Although Capri is suitable for simply strolling, relaxing, dining, and people-watching, it's easy to find all of the locations mentioned above. Once you arrive on the island, hop on the funicular up to the main town of Capri and set off on one of the numerous pedestrian pathways spreading out from the main piazza.

VILLA CIMBRONE

The Amalfi Drive...this famed section of the Italian coastline south of Naples has inspired visitors for thousands of years. Even the Caesars of ancient Rome knew that the sunsplashed rocky coastline could soothe the most tempestuous soul.

Fast forward 1,400 years to an era when the great naval powers of Naples and Venice and Genoa dominated the commercial world. Amazingly, tiny little Amalfi held its own in that era, generating enough wealth for the local citizenry to build a beautiful church that speaks, even today, of that commercial prowess.

By the nineteenth and twentieth centuries, Amalfi's former glory was gone. However, the magnificent scenery remained just as enticing, and wealthy citizens began to take advantage of the spectacular views from just about everywhere. Villas with drop-dead views began to sprout and, today, you, the lucky visitor, can bed down overnight in those that became hotels or just visit for lunch or dinner.

High above Amalfi in the even sleepier town of Ravello lies Villa Cimbrone, perched on the edge of a rocky outcropping overlooking the sparkling Mediterranean Sea far below. A historic structure, parts of the villa date back to the eleventh century. By the twelfth century, it had become the home of a wealthy local family, passing through several more aristocratic owners. In 1904, its modern history began when Ernest Beckett bought it and began to restore the villa, and most importantly, its gardens.

With the help of a local barber/builder, Beckett constructed and restored battlements, terraces, and a cloister in a mixture of mock-Gothic, Moorish, and Venetian architectural styles. He lavished attention on the gardens, strung out along the cliff face.

Because of his connections with the literary world of England, many famous writers and artists began to visit the villa and marvel at its exquisite gardens. The Bloomsbury Group from London, including Virginia Woolf, Leonard Woolf, E. M. Forster, John Maynard Keynes, and Lytton Strachey, were all visitors. D. H. Lawrence, Vita Sackville-West, Edward James, Diana Mosley, Henry Moore, T. S. Eliot, Jean Piaget, Winston Churchill, and the Duke and

Duchess of Kent spent time there. The actress Greta Garbo and her then-lover, the conductor Leopold Stokowski, stayed at the villa several times in the late 1930s; her visit of 1938 is memorialized on a plaque.

The modern gardens owe much to Vita Sackville-West. Interestingly, she blended the English love of flowers and open green spaces with the Renaissance Italian ethos of a "noble" garden. Thus, you will find a rose garden and other beautiful floral plantings married to flat emerald-green terraces, separated by greenery, water, and stone into discrete sections at slightly different elevations. Your eye is always drawn to another section waiting to be explored. Classical elements such as a small Temple of Bacchus and marble statues punctuate the natural components so that man and nature are combined. Eventually, all visitors end up at the cliff-edge walkway titled the Terrace of Infinity, where Roman statues are placed just so. To gaze out over the land below to the endless sea from the Terrace of Infinity can only be described as magical.

To give you a sense of the entrancing combination of sea, sky, gardens and history, the writer Gore Vidal (who lived nearby in Ravello) wrote, "Twenty-five years ago I was asked by an American magazine what was the most beautiful place that I had ever seen in all my travels, and I said the view from the belvedere of the Villa Cimbrone on a bright winter's day when the sky and the sea were each so vividly blue that it was not possible to tell one from the other."

The villa now survives as a luxury hotel, but the gardens are open to the public for a small fee. Alternatively, reserve a table for lunch on the beautiful hotel terrace. Add a glass of white wine as you dine on the excellent fare at a leisurely pace. The stillness and the serenity of your clifftop location enhance the overall experience.

Afterward, you can stroll in the gardens. As you gaze out into the endless blue of the sky and sea, I'm sure you will reflect on life and its meaning. It's that kind of place.

THE DEATH OF JULIUS CAESAR

The assassination of Julius Caesar in 44 BCE ranks among the most famous events in history. Everything from the number of stab wounds (twenty-three) to his famous last words to his erstwhile friend, Brutus, (*Et tu, Brute?*) has been borne through the dusty pages of history to the modern age. School age children can easily recite the facts and the man's dying words. And there's a certain morbid fascination with the prophetic warning, "Beware the Ides of March," isn't there?

How about watching a dramatic reenactment in the place where it all happened, more than 2,000 years ago? In recent years, a local historical society devoted to classic Roman history has staged just such an event in the Largo di Torre Argentina on March 15th, the Ides of March.

Largo di Torre Argentina is NOT in the Roman Forum where the Roman Senate, the Curia, was located. At the time of the assassination, the Senate was meeting in Pompey's Theater while the Curia underwent renovation. Thus, the Senators staged their "intervention" close to the Senate's temporary meeting place, now part of Largo Argentina.

The commemoration occurs in three scenes. The participants don classical Roman garb to enhance the scene. You'll see togas, a crown of laurel leaves for the great man himself, and sandals.

The first scene portrays Marc Antony, Cato, Cicero, senators, and tribunes of the people meeting to discuss the "situation" in the Senate. After almost five hundred years of the Republic, Julius Caesar had broken the bounds of democracy, brought his army across the Rubicon River into the city of Rome (which had been forbidden), and seized dictatorial powers. Of course, he said it was all done to safeguard the Republic, but dictators always say things just like that. The peril to the Republic could no longer be ignored or excused. Now, the protagonists of the Senate must meet to figure out what to do next and how to save the Republic. At the end of the scene, the Senators declare Caesar a public enemy of Rome.

In the second scene, Caesar arrives in the Senate and meets a fortune teller who warns him: "Caesar, beware the Ides of March!" It is unclear if Caesar really did receive such a warning, but an account by Plutarch indicates he was indeed advised just so. William Shakespeare thought the information was solid enough to include the encounter in his play *Julius Caesar*. Ergo, the warning has been incorporated into historical lore and this reenactment.

After the warning, the assassination duly occurs. Many members of the Senate each take their turn with a knife to assault Caesar. History tells us that about forty conspirators lunged at him and at least twenty-three thrusts went home. Brutus delivers the final one, at which point Caesar utters his plaintive cry of betrayal, "Even you, Brutus?" Caesar lurches from stab to stab in a very dramatic fashion, illustrating just how violent and bloody the murder was.

The third and final scene presents the funeral at which the eloquent and moving speeches of Brutus and Mark Antony from the Shakespeare play command center stage. "Friends, Romans, Countrymen, lend me your ears. I have come to bury Caesar, not to praise him." Even now, those stirring words pose an age-old question: Is violence justified when the result of inaction means an even worse outcome? No easy answers then or now...

The reenactment usually begins at around 1:30 or 2:00 pm. You do not need a ticket and you can watch from the street. Speeches are in Italian, of course, but the action speaks for itself.

MUSSOLINI'S FASCIST ARCHITECTURE TOWN

Whether or not Benito Mussolini made the trains run on time in Italy is a matter of dispute; most Italians disagree. And today, Mussolini deservedly belongs in the "ashheap of history." It is hard to imagine the devastation wreaked upon Italy because of his leadership. In this day and age, tourists flock to the vine-covered hills of Tuscany or the rocky shoreline of the spectacular Amalfi Coast for vacations in gorgeous surroundings.

But you can see remnants of Mussolini's grandiose plans to restore Italy to the glory of the Roman empire in the fascist architecture that he endorsed and promoted during his dictatorship. The Galleria and the Central Train Station in Milan get the most attention. But the small town of Sabaudia encapsulates both the power that he exercised as well as the "concepts" that he translated into buildings.

Beginning in the 1920s, the dictator decided to show off Italian engineering capabilities by draining the malaria-infested Pontine marshes about sixty miles south of Rome on the coast. He imported more than six thousand impoverished workers from northern Italy to do the work. He originally intended that the land would be used for agriculture. However, as the years passed and he grew more and more ambitious, he decided to create an entirely new town, Sabaudia.

After an architectural contest, the three winning architects designed Sabaudia on a classic Roman grid. Construction began on August 5, 1933 and finished 253 days later. The architects sought to incorporate classic Italian urban design with the demands for modern "greatness" envisioned by their dictator patron.

Were they successful? Fascist architecture invariably hewed towards big and blocky. Massive. Powerful. Imposing. And that's exactly what you'll see in Sabaudia.

Here, interpreting the needs of any Italian population, the architects created a Town Hall with a 150-foot-high tower, a central piazza for the population to gather in, and a covered market, as well as the church of SS. Annunziata. The Town

Hall tower affords fine views over the town and countryside.

That church? It sure doesn't look like St. Peter's in Rome. In addition to its basic blocky form, its décor consists of a mosaic, the top part of which depicts the Annunciation. The bottom part displays common episodes of rural life, with Mussolini himself in the act of arranging wheat sheaves. The adjacent Baptistry, the 150-foot bell tower and the Presbytery with an internal courtyard seek to evoke the atmosphere of a traditional medieval square.

The most interesting building is the startling Post Office, which now houses a museum illustrating the story of Sabaudia. Its facade sports blue Savoy tiles with a red Siena marble border around the large windows, which open onto the central hall. A wide external staircase leads to the living quarters for the former Postmaster. Oh yes, Mussolini went full Modern on this one while still seeking to link himself to the former ruling family, the Savoys.

Across the street sits the Royal Carabinieri barracks, and nearby you will find the Casa del Fascio (former local Fascist HQ) with an interesting turret and large connecting porticoes and buildings. The locals demolished the original covered market years ago to create Piazza Santa Barbara.

Other buildings of interest include the School and Opera Nazionale Balilla (the former Fascist youth organization), the movie theater, the barracks of the Voluntary Militia for National Security, and the local health center, formerly the Hospital and Maternity Center.

Long after Mussolini's demise, this seaside location began to attract artists and filmmakers. Today, despite the association with fascism, the low-rise buildings lend a human scale to the town. Red brick, travertine, and yellow stucco facades line the palm-studded streets, and it's not hard to understand why those of artistic sensibilities were drawn here. You'll find not only film stars but also media heads and even some Russian oligarchs.

As you stroll through the town, you can see the remnants of the town's origins. If you ascend the Town Hall Tower, look at the bell, inscribed with the fascist eagles above the rods from which the word fascism derives. On a wall, you may see a faint stencil with the word *vincere* (to conquer). And on the church mosaic, don't forget the misplaced image of Mussolini bundling wheat sheaves together.

For your best experience, absolutely spend some money to hire a private guide who can give you the context you need to understand what happened here and the vestiges of this unusual town's origins.

AMALFI COAST BOAT TOUR

Many travelers have heard of the magical Amalfi Coast. South of Naples, on the west coast of Italy, this small peninsula juts out into the Mediterranean and the Bay of Naples. The town of Sorrento lies on the top of a triangle of land, and if you travel up and over the hill, the road brings you down to Positano and, eventually, Amalfi. These two towns define the glorious Amalfi Coast, and the road between justly earns every bit of fame as one of the most beautiful drives in the world.

In truth, the spectacular coastal scenery is not a secret, and every summer, visitors flock to the region to soak up the sun, smell the lemons, gaze out at the sea crashing on the rocks below, and people-watch in the small cafes and bars dotting the landscape. Experienced travelers know the tight dimensions of that two-lane road along the coast. If you, in your rental car, encounter the local bus coming the other way around the bend in the road, you will have to stop and carefully back up until the bus can squeeze by you. And there are lots of cars right behind you.

There IS a better way to experience the Amalfi Coast in the peak summer months of July and August. Hire a private boat and see the coast from the cobalt waters of the Mediterranean Sea! The views are gorgeous from the water.

The marinas of Sorrento, Positano, and Amalfi offer numerous small boats for full- or half-day charters. When you arrive in town, either ask your hotel concierge for a contact or head down to the waterfront to make the arrangements for an upcoming day. The weather is usually excellent in that part of Italy during the summer months, but you can certainly escape a rainy day, if necessary.

Offshore, you'll find yourself amid the sparkling, crystalline waters of the Mediterranean. Has anyone told you how far down you can see? Very far in those clear blue waters.

A good itinerary would certainly take you along the coast to see glittering Positano. The town straddles two adjacent hills and the image looks as if someone designed a picture-perfect village, ready for its postcard "close-up"—and then built the town to match the postcard afterwards. Then, on to little Amalfi—a faded relic of its former glory days when it rivaled Venice and Genoa as a major shipping power. The wealth generated by the shipping paid for the beautiful cathedral, and you'll see the rays of the sun glinting off the gold dome at the top. Along the way between Amalfi and Positano, coastal viewers can spy the little, teeny towns between them, barely visible from the road. Minori even shows the remains of a Roman villa from the first century. Only from the sea can the remains of the residential buildings be seen, since the other buildings were eventually used as wineries in the succeeding centuries.

And now, your boat turns towards the mythical island of Capri. Its Blue Grotto has dazzled visitors with its unearthly light for years and years. Warning: the summer months see hours-long waits to get into the grotto. You can check with your captain to decide if this is a good use of your time. Perhaps you'll focus on the Coral Grotto or sail under the Stone Arch instead. Blue Grotto or not, as you gaze upwards, you'll see that just two towns dot the hills: Capri and AnaCapri; naturally, the residents don't get along!

As you circumnavigate the glorious rocky coastline, you'll see the waves crashing on those rocks, throwing up white foam everywhere. Contrasted with the sparkling blue water, the view is just indescribably gorgeous.

You'll pass by the rocks from which the famous Sirens lured sailors to their deaths. Their haunting melodies caused passing crews to jump into the sea where they drowned. Remember that Odysseus told his crew to tie him to the mast so that he could hear the song and live to tell about it. This legend is reflected today in the numerous restaurants and hotels of Positano and Sorrento that bear the name *Syrene* or *Le Sirene* or some variation thereon.

Whether you choose a three-hour coastal cruise or a full-day sail, you'll skip a crowded road full of traffic in favor of a relaxing day in some of the most beautiful waters on this earth. And a sunset return is magical.

Note: *Even if you haven't chartered your own boat, you can always hop on the hydrofoil from Sorrento down to Positano and Amalfi and enjoy some of those wonderful views. An evening return with the moon over the coastal hills is pretty darn romantic!*

WATER ORGAN CONCERT AT THE VILLA D'ESTE

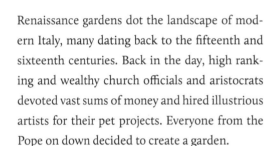

Renaissance gardens dot the landscape of modern Italy, many dating back to the fifteenth and sixteenth centuries. Back in the day, high ranking and wealthy church officials and aristocrats devoted vast sums of money and hired illustrious artists for their pet projects. Everyone from the Pope on down decided to create a garden.

Italy's most famous garden is the magnificent Villa d'Este in Tivoli, about ten miles west of Rome. Not to be confused with the famous hotel of the same name at Lake Como, the Villa d'Este in Tivoli does have a lovely palace to stroll through, but it's the gardens that rightfully draw the visitors.

In 1560, Cardinal Ippolito d'Este began its construction, hiring hundreds of laborers to dig out a hillside by hand (no earth digging equipment or motors in that era). With the design and input of a prominent architect, he installed an incredible system of pipes to feed water from the top of the hill to wherever he chose.

The Villa d'Este speaks about water: water cascading down hillsides, water shooting high up in powerful jets, water arcing over sculptures, water flowing through terraces, water gently lapping in a series of reflecting pools. In all, in this one garden, you can find fifty-one fountains and nymphaeums, 398 spouts, 364 water jets, 64 waterfalls, and 220 basins fed by 2,800 feet of canals, channels, and cascades all working entirely by the force of gravity, without pumps.

Significantly, you will also find the Water Organ Fountain, an organ that uses water to activate air in the pipes to play—and yes, it still works. It was the first of its kind and it astonished everyone who heard it. When Pope Gregory XIII visited the villa in 1572, accompanied by his court of cardinals and princes, he insisted on inspecting the interior of the fountain to learn if someone wasn't concealed inside making the music.

A massive masonry arch behind the fountain, the *castellum aquae* or water castle, conceals a water reservoir and the hydraulic machinery of the fountain. Originally, twenty-two pipes were fed by water that arrived first at the top of the *castellum aquae*. A series of whirlpools mixed air with the water before it dropped down a pipe into a wind chamber, where the air and water were separated again. The water turned a wheel, rotating a cylinder, opening the valves of the twenty-two pipes so that air could pass through the pipes and make the music.

Of course, a number of centuries have passed since 1571 and, over time, the water organ and its amazing machinery decayed. There were lengthy periods of neglect and without constant cleaning and maintenance, it was difficult to keep the organ operational. Several times, restorations revived the organ, including one in the 1700s that increased the number of pipes to 144. However, by the end of that century, repair was no longer feasible.

And so, the organ sat, mute, for more than two hundred years. Happily for you, the garden administrators (with a lot of funding) undertook a delicate and very serious restoration, completed in 2003. The restorers were able to retain the original wind chamber and tank for creating whirlpools, while they replaced the rest of the mechanism with new modern machinery that follows the original principles of design. A cylinder controls the 144 pipes, still set in motion by the water.

And the performance? First, the gates covering the pipes open. A triumphant blare sounds, followed by silence, and then another triumphant blare. Having grabbed your attention, the hidden organist embarks on four pieces of late Renaissance music. It's recognizable and sounds just like an organ should. For a total of four minutes, you can picture old-style ladies and lords dancing a stately quadrille in their aristocratic finery, accompanied by this ethereal music from the past.

The architecture around the water organ is ornate, not surprising given that additional elements were added during the Baroque era. You'll see niches, statues, columns, arches, and bas-reliefs, and even a stone falcon, the symbol of the Este family.

The massive water organ sits above the Fountain of Neptune, the largest and most spectacular fountain in the gardens. The fountain features two powerful water jets shooting upwards as high as forty-five feet, flanked by six smaller jets of varying height which originate from a higher level of the fountain. The Neptune Fountain also includes a series of seven water cascades, on different terraces, with different shapes and orientations. It finishes in a series of three tranquil reflecting pools.

The Neptune Fountain and the Fountain of the Water Organ together form a complex, nearly eighty feet high and sixty-seven feet wide. The sound of the rushing water is loud and impressive and magnetically draws us humans close to its borders.

In summer, the Villa d'Este and its gardens are open from 8:30 am to 7:30 pm. In winter, the gardens close earlier. As a rule, the organ plays every two hours, beginning at 10:30 am.

THE REGATA STORICA

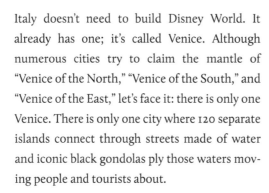

Italy doesn't need to build Disney World. It already has one; it's called Venice. Although numerous cities try to claim the mantle of "Venice of the North," "Venice of the South," and "Venice of the East," let's face it: there is only one Venice. There is only one city where 120 separate islands connect through streets made of water and iconic black gondolas ply those waters moving people and tourists about.

Most of us know that the city's highlights include the magnificent Piazza San Marco, the Doge's Palace with the Bridge of Sighs, the three bridges spanning the Grand Canal, and the beautiful Byzantine-style Basilica San Marco. In truth, part of the city's charm is simply being there and strolling the backways and tiny streets and crossing those endless little bridges. Everyone can find their own private Venice.

This remarkable city has always gloried in spectacle and parties. You've probably heard that Carnevale di Venezia sets the standard for Mardi Gras celebrations every winter. But wait, there's more.

Once a year, the local citizens dust off their Renaissance heritage to present the past in living color. And what a glorious past it was—and, of course, boats underpinned everything.

Venice dominated the Adriatic coastlines for several hundred years during the Renaissance, and the city grew rich and fat on its shipping prowess. The doges (the local rulers or dukes) enjoyed their luxuries while badly oppressing the citizens. They built the beautiful Doge's Palace and the gorgeous Piazza San Marco while their "friends" enjoyed their own beautiful palazzos along the Grand Canal. When the doges needed to leave that palace and visit their friends, they traveled in style on princely gondolas. Of course, the doges' era ended a very long time ago, but Venice has not forgotten the old days.

On the First Sunday in September, the city sponsors the Regata Storica. As you can guess from the name Regata, this one-day festival involves boats. All day long, racing crews test their spirit, mettle, and strength on the Grand

Canal. To kick off the day of fun and sport, the Venetians dig out the ceremonial boats of the past and sail them down the Grand Canal.

Perch yourself on a convenient post along the Grand Canal to watch the parade of historic gondolas and ceremonial boats. Modest vessels with crews of four rowers will float by. You'll see more impressive, bigger boats, with six-man crews. Finally, you'll goggle at the boats of the doges with eight or even twelve-man crews.

Remember: The doges acted as the local kings. Their princely vessels needed to impress the local populace, and they surely did. Elaborate gilded carvings decorate the doges' boats on the prow, the stern, and the sides. Polished and gleaming, the carvings contrast against the black lacquer wood of the stately vessels. Most of the crews sport matching Renaissance costumes of rich reds, greens, blues, and golds, even while they haul away on those oars. Even today, you, the humble spectator, can't help but be impressed at all that glory sailing by.

The races last for hours and, depending on your enthusiasm, you might want to spend your day watching them. However, a little racing goes a long way, so feel free to resume your happy wandering in this very special city on a very special day.

While Venice has lost its glory as a Renaissance shipping power, the Regata Storica brings it all back for one shining moment.

JAPAN

KYOTO
OSAKA
SEKI

SUMO WRESTLING EXPERIENCE

Sumo wrestling makes some of our world's most arresting competitions. The oversized bodies, the minimalist clothing (as in loincloth only), the grunting, and the sheer physicality of the sport make it hard to look away.

Arising in ancient times, the first "wrestlers" were actually performing Shinto ritual dances to display strength in front of the *kami* (gods or spirits) as a sign of respect and gratitude to bring in a good harvest. Today, sumo still relies heavily on ritual, and it remains a men-only sport for professionals.

How does sumo work? The idea is to stay within the *dohyō* (ring) and to touch the ground with only the soles of your feet. The first man to exit the ring or touch the ground with any other part of the body loses. Pretty simple, right? Since there are no weight classes, the bigger you are, the more of an advantage you possess against your opponent. Thus, weight gain is an integral part of the sumo wrestling training regimen.

Now that you understand how to compete, time to get into the ring yourself! In this sumo experience, you will enjoy a short demonstration and explanation of the sport and its practices. Then, "volunteers" can face off against retired wrestlers in a ring, wearing a traditional costume. (Your opponent will wear the typical loincloth with belt.)

It is helpful to understand the rites that all *rikishi* (sumo wrestlers) perform before a bout. Wrestlers generally have about four minutes before a match during which to prepare.

To add authenticity to your own match, you may want to extend your arms vigorously. Perhaps you should stamp your feet (*shiko*). And squat a few times. Or glare meaningfully at your opponent. This is the time when opponents will toss handfuls of salt into the air to purify the ring. *Rikishi* then receive the *chikara mizu* and *chikara gami* (power water and power paper) from another wrestler. Finally, there are a series of moves performed to demonstrate that the wrestlers are not carrying a weapon.

During your demonstration bout, be aware that you may NOT grab your opponent's belt to try to throw him down. You may not try to push or lift your opponent out of the ring. You may not try to trip him by the legs or jump quickly off to one side. You may not slap him or try to save yourself from falling out of the ring digging into the straw at the edge of the ring.

Sumo wrestling is still a sport only practiced by men. Do be sensitive to local customs and let the men in your group do the wrestling. Everyone else will want to have their cameras ready.

TEA CEREMONY AND PRIVATE VISIT TO MASAKI ART MUSEUM

The Masaki Art Museum near Osaka preserves the private collection of Takayuki Masaki, one of the most important art collectors in Japan in the post-World War II era. Among the 1,300 pieces of art and artifacts displayed are three National Treasures of Japan and thirteen Important Cultural Properties.

Mr. Masaki built many factories as Japan began to recover from the devastation of the war, and he began to collect art, as well. He was particularly interested in ink wash drawings and paintings dating from the Kamakura (1185–1333) and Muromachi (1336–1573) periods (the Japanese Middle Ages).

Your private visit to the museum includes not only a guided tour with a docent who can explain the significance of the various objects, but also a special tea ceremony. Because Mr. Masaki was interested in the classical Japanese tea traditions, his collection includes a 400-year-old portrait of the most famous tea master in Japanese history, Rikyū. Although the image of a geisha pouring tea for her guest is well known, the origins of this cultural tradition are much deeper than this somewhat simplified image.

Rikyū was a tea master who lived in the 1500s near Kyoto, and he established many of the formal elements of the tea ceremony still used today. He was already fifty-eight years old when he needed some credentials in order to assist at a tea ceremony given by a famous samurai (Hideyoshi) for the emperor. The emperor bestowed upon him the Buddhist lay name and title "Rikyū Koji."

Because of his entry into the world of the emperor, he began to codify the elements of this all-important tea ritual.

He began to use very tiny, rustic tea rooms referred to as a "grass hermitage." With room for just two tatami mats, these tea rooms are credited to his design and have been designated a National Treasure. He also developed many implements for the tea ceremony, including flower containers, tea scoops, and lid rests made of bamboo. However, Rikyū also used everyday objects for the tea ceremony, often in novel ways. With a preference for simple rustic items made in Japan, Rikyū worked with a tile-maker to design Raku teabowls.

Though not the inventor of the philosophy of wabi-sabi, which finds beauty in simplicity, Rikyū is among those most responsible for popularizing it, developing it, and incorporating it into the tea ceremony. He created a new form of the tea ritual using very simple instruments and surroundings. This whole belief system and his teachings came to be known as sōan-cha (the grass-thatched hermitage style of chanoyu), or more generally, "wabi-cha."

Although Rikyū's rise to fame ensured his legacy five hundred years later, sadly he fell out of favor with his patron, the famous samurai Hideyoshi. In fact, Hideyoshi ordered him to commit *seppuku* (suicide by dagger), and Rikyū complied. According to *The Book of Tea*, Rikyū's last act was to hold an exquisite tea ceremony. After serving all his guests, he presented each piece of the tea implements for their inspection, along with an exquisite *kakemono*, described as "a wonderful writing by an ancient monk dealing with the evanescence of all things."

Each of his guests was given a piece of the equipment as a souvenir, with the exception of the bowl, which he shattered as he uttered the words: "Never again shall this cup, polluted by the lips of misfortune, be used by man." As the guests departed, one remained to serve as witness to Rikyū's death. Rikyū's last words, which he wrote down as a death poem, were in verse, addressed to the dagger with which he took his own life:

Welcome to thee,
O sword of eternity!
Through Buddha
And through Daruma alike
Thou hast cleft thy way.

After the tea ceremony, your guide will explain the museum's collection as it relates to the multi-faceted process of serving and consuming tea in Japan.

THE ART OF THE SAMURAI SWORD

The *katana* (samurai) sword underpins the entire Japanese culture of the samurai warrior. Featured in countless books and movies (and timeless John Belushi skits on SNL), samurai warriors evoke a highly ritualized society with strict rules of behavior, detailed codes of honor and insult, and highly disciplined and lengthy training. Before your immersion into sword-making, a little background...

Harkening back to the eleventh century, samurai swords evolved from short blades to the longer style that could be quickly drawn for use in hand-to-hand combat. By the time the Tokugawa shogunate dominated Japan in the 1800s, the rules surrounding the use and display of the swords had become highly stylized.

The shogun required samurai to wear *katana* and shorter swords in pairs. These short swords were *wakizashi* and *tantō*, with this set of two called a *daishō*. Only samurai could wear the *daishō* since it represented social power and personal honor.

Samurai could wear decorative sword mountings in their daily lives, but the Tokugawa shogunate regulated the formal sword that samurai wore when visiting a castle. The *daishō* had to consist of the two swords, a black scabbard, and a hilt wrapped with white ray skin and black string.

As we conceive of the samurai warrior today, he is defined and represented by his *katana*, the curved, single-edged blade which means "big sword." The classic *katana* is almost twenty-four inches long and is worn, blade side up, by the samurai warrior.

In the town of Seki, slightly north of Nagoya on Honshu, you can learn about the interplay of religion, warriorship, and craftmanship inherent in the making of the *katana*. The craftsmen of this village have been making highly prized swords for seven hundred years.

Many different elements comprise the traditional *katana*, beginning with the metal used for the blade. A *tosho*, the swordsmith, is a master blacksmith who painstakingly harnesses an immense heat of 1,300 degrees Celsius to forge carbon steel blades. By the color of the flame and the sound of the iron, a *tosho* battles the spirit of the flame to fuse soft iron between harder iron plates.

In addition, a *habaki* maker (or shiroganeshi) focuses on chiseling the *habaki*, a metal collar made of gold, silver, or bronze that sits at the hilt of the katana. This intricate work requires hours of painstaking, steady handiwork, although the *habaki* is a very small piece of metal.

Each *katana* is also adorned with a *tsukamaki*, a hand-fitted cord around the hilt. By varying the turns and tension of the cord, the minute details within the interlocking pattern mark the expertise of a seasoned *tsukamakishi* artisan.

Don't forget the sword polisher, *togishi*. The *togishi* spend hours of work polishing the *katana* to bring it to its utmost sharpness. The look and feel of the sword will tell the *togishi* when the finished product is polished and ready.

And of course, the *katana* has a scabbard or sheath to protect it while not in use. The *sayashi* specializes in chiseling the scabbard for each sword out of the finest wood. Fastened by a glue made of sticky rice, the one-of-a-kind scabbard cradles the finished *katana* perfectly. Beneath the *sayashi* is an ever-growing pile of wood shavings, of course.

After you meet with these *katana* craftsmen and learn the intricacy of this incredible tradition, you can ask questions through an interpreter. And you can even try hammering out a blade. Hint: It's harder than it looks.

Now the truly fun part: your *iaigiri* training session. Have your partner get the camera ready while you don a traditional *iai* outfit and channel your inner John Belushi. A certified expert will show you how to swing the sword, and then it's your turn. Take a few swings at a bamboo target, not another samurai! Good luck.

After your visit to Seki, I guarantee that you'll never look at a movie samurai the same way again.

JORDAN

JERASH

ROMAN CHARIOT RACING

Who doesn't love a good chariot race? And who dominated the field of chariot racing? You know the answer: the Romans.

As you will recall from elementary school, the Roman Empire covered most of the Mediterranean at its peak, including what we now call the Middle East. In exchange for loyalty and monetary tribute to the Empire coffers, the Romans endowed their subject peoples with amphitheaters, art, aqueducts, and entertainment. Admittedly, the entertainment tended towards swords and sandals, but the locals seemed to like it just fine.

While most visitors to Jordan head straight to Petra with its stunning rock carved temples, consider adding a visit to Jerash for an afternoon of entertainment, Roman style. About an hour north of Amman, Jerash houses only about 50,000 inhabitants today. However, in Roman times, its location along major trade routes made it a wealthy and important town. The Emperor Hadrian actually "wintered" here one year. The relics of its heyday are well preserved and impressive and include Hadrian's Arch, the Corinthian columns of the Temple of Artemis, and a huge oval colonnade of its forum.

Some years ago, an enterprising businessman decided to pay homage to his favorite film *Ben-Hur* by embracing the city's Roman heritage. Specifically, he decided to stage chariot races in the ancient style. Over the years, the concept evolved into a broader performance incorporating the other "popular" aspects of Roman life. A shaded seat in the hippodrome gives you a chance to channel your inner Augustus Caesar.

The Roman Army and Chariot Experience begins with a man in armor blowing a horn. Forty-five Roman legionaries march into the ancient hippodrome, clad in their armor, helmets, and sandals. They take up a fair amount of room and they raise a cloud of dust in the hot, sandy space. Although this legion comprises forty-five warriors, historians can never agree whether a Roman legion numbered three hundred men or three thousand. But why quibble?

In battle formation, the legionnaires raise their spears and their shields. Their battle lines form and reform, demonstrating strength and discipline against all comers, whether infantry or cavalry. Imagine how effectively the power projection instilled a sense of futility for any locals considering resistance. After a little more strutting and posing, the phalanx disperses as gladiators enter the arena.

In traditional gladiator garb, the "prisoners" and "scum" show off their various skills. After all, gladiators came in all shapes and sizes. Actually, size-wise, the guys all display pretty beefy physiques. Some use swords while others use nets and tridents, but the goal is always the same. Kill the other guy so that you can live one more day.

You'll hear a lot of grunting and moaning, as some of the fighters go down to defeat and others raise their hands in victory after they (pretend to) drive the sword home in the final moment of the fight. Of course, no one really dies in these demonstrations, but the grappling and sword thrusting look pretty authentic.

After the gladiators have finished their bouts and demonstrations, the main event gears up— the chariot race. So, what do you need to know about chariot-racing, Roman-style?

First, racing teams are color-coded. As a fan, you'll want to easily identify and cheer on your favorite driver(s). Some things never change.

Second, chariots are very fragile. A simple collision can result in immediate destruction of chariot, horses, and driver. The drivers are brave men. The stakes are high; the driver's life could end suddenly. A chariot race is a bumpy ride on wooden wheels and taking the corners of the racing oval at high speed threatens a spill every time.

Third, in the olden days, teams actually used four chariots each. Most of the chariots were drawn by four horses and the charioteers needed to complete seven laps of the arena to win. Today's chariots generally use two horses, but they still must complete seven laps. Each performance includes several races.

Since no one wants to witness injury or worse to either drivers or animals, the performance uses only well-trained drivers and horses. Injuries are rare and animal lovers need not fear a spectacle that would cause distress.

Note: *The photography in* Ben-Hur's *chariot race put you in the center of the high-speed and brutal action. Watching from the stands is not quite as thrilling as being IN the chariot, fearing that your competitor's wheel spokes will cut off your chariot's wheels and cause you to quit—or better yet, suffer death. Aside from that, a live chariot race offers a lot of fun.*

In Jerash, the ancient arena could seat 15,000 spectators, attesting to the eternal popularity of this ancient sport. That's actually on the small side for a Roman arena, but it means that you'll enjoy a great view of the competition.

"Ave, Imperator. Morituri Te Salutamus." Translation: Hail, Emperor. We who are about to die salute you.

MEXICO

PUEBLA

TILE PAINTING WORKSHOP

The brightly colored ceramic tiles of Mexico brighten up many a room and home in the United States. The shiny cobalt blues contrast with bright reds and yellows making for an eye-pleasing palette of rainbow colors.

The tiles' heritage harks back to the age of the European explorers and the Spanish Conquistadors. Shortly after the Conquistadors carved out a foothold in the New World, the Catholic church sent forth its emissaries. To cement the Christian influence, the local priests built churches in Mexico—lots of them; an estimated 365 of them!

The church fathers drew upon the largesse of wealthy Spanish landowners in these new lands as they began to adorn the new buildings. In and around Puebla, founded in 1531, the fathers built over seventy churches. The new settlers hired local artisans to decorate them with tiles, giving rise to the Talavera Poblana style of pottery.

Building on the ceramic skills and traditions found in Talavera de la Reina in Spain, Talavera Poblana evolved into highly prized pottery. The local clay was of particularly good quality and the sheer number of churches meant a steady supply of customers. The artisans were particularly fond of blue for their tiles, although colors such as yellow, black, green, orange, and mauve are also considered authentic. The streets of Puebla offer myriad charming pieces of pottery at lots of different price levels.

If you'd like to try your hand at this unique art form, stop in at Uriarte Talavera, the largest fabricator of Talavera pottery in all of Latin America, for a private tour and pottery workshop. This Puebla factory, housed in the original home of Don Ignacio Uriarte, operated as a family workshop until the 1990s.

A private tour of the factory lets you understand the lengthy process by which water and clay transform into these beautiful objects, some for everyday use, some to brighten up kitchen walls, and others to sit as art pieces.

First, you will see how the mud and water mix. Next, the tile makers mold the clay by hand into all the various shapes and sizes that pottery encompasses. Once the shapes meet the standards set by the artisans, the raw pieces sit drying for several weeks before they are loaded into the kilns for the first time. After the pieces have been fired, the artisans apply enamel to the raw clay.

At last, they begin the process of decoration. First, they trace the intricate designs on each object in stencils. This painstaking work allows for precise coloration of these complex patterns. The simplest ones feature blocky flowers in the center with accents on the borders. Others draw on the geometric intricacy of a kaleidoscope mirror. Still others feature concentric rings of varying colors and shapes. No two tiles look the same, and they're not supposed to.

Once the stencils have been traced onto the pieces, the artisans begin to paint, coloring in the designs just so. The pigments derive from local natural ingredients such ochre, cobalt, and copper oxide. After the artists have finished painting, each piece goes back into the kiln for its second and final firing. The result: a decorative tile featuring vibrant hues of blue and green and gold and red.

Now, it's your turn. Put on your smock and prepare to apply your skills and your design ideas to a blank pottery "canvas." During the tile painting workshop, you will learn the principles of authentic decoration from a pottery master. And, of course, you can bring your tile home with you!

NEW ZEALAND

QUEENSTOWN
ROTORUA

DART RIVER VALLEY BY JETBOAT

Queenstown, at the bottom of New Zealand's South Island, attracts all kinds of adventure enthusiasts eager to bungee jump, experience the thrill of the Shotover Canyon Jetboat ride, heli-ski, skydive, bike, hike, and enjoy numerous other outdoor pursuits. As you amble down the streets of this beautiful sub-alpine town, you'll encounter countless tour shops with sandwich boards advertising the incredible local activities on offer.

Not all of us are daredevils, of course. Can a less adventurous soul find great activities in Queenstown? Absolutely. The drive over to Milford Sound to experience that glorious fjord certainly counts. But the Dart River Valley excursion should also command your attention.

Setting off from Queenstown, you'll follow the shores of stunning Lake Wakatipu to its northern end where you'll pass through the small town of Glenorchy, perched at the foot of the Dart River valley. Just a few shops and modest inns make up Glenorchy, but a convenient rest stop serves up light fare and features a good shop for local products. Manuka honey, anyone?

Now, the day gets a little *Lord of the Rings*-ish. Still traveling by road, you'll pass through lush green meadows where numerous scenes from the trilogy were filmed. If you're on a guided tour, your tour leader will stop at a certain point to show you stills from not only LOTR movies, but also *Narnia* and other well-known films, while pointing to the specific film locations all around you.

Finally, you are ready to board a small jetboat for just twelve passengers. This jetboat does not focus on giving you a thrill ride. Save that for the Shotover Canyon. Instead, understand that only a jetboat can access the innermost reaches of this gorgeous valley. Shallow channels of water only a few inches deep allow for navigation by highly skilled jetboat pilots. The rivulets shift this way and that over pebbles and rocks, each and every day. No two routes will be the same. The jetboat pilots have trained long and hard to negotiate the shifting channels so that you can penetrate deep into the valley, skimming over the fragile waterways.

On every side you'll look up at snow-capped mountain peaks. Craggy outcroppings define the valley walls. White waterfalls accent steeper rockfaces. Hidden, verdant, and quiet glens beckon you to diverge from the main channel if enough water permits it. Perhaps your driver will cut the engine here while everyone savors the incredible natural beauty all around you. Voices are naturally soft and gentle here, as if to let the dramatic landscape penetrate your soul.

Eventually, it will be time to find new channels to take you back downstream to the opening of Lake Wakatipu at Glenorchy, and eventually your return to Queenstown.

Don't bother taking pictures; no camera can really capture the scenes of alpine meadows, rocky crags, glistening water, and waterfalls. Like seeing the Grand Canyon, you just have to be there.

STEAMBOX LUNCH AT TE PUIA

Did you know that New Zealand is bubbling away in a geothermal stew? Maybe not. Does the name Geothermal Highway give you a clue? It should. This land is vibrantly alive.

After you arrive in Auckland on North Island (where the big international airport is), drive south about three hours on the Geothermal Highway to the small town of Rotorua. Rotorua serves as a great base for visiting Hobbiton and the Waitomo Glowworm Caves and for experiencing Maori traditional ways of life. Importantly, the area around Rotorua boasts the largest collection of geysers, bubbling mud pots, steam vents, and sulfur pools in the world. You can smell the lake before you get there.

On the edge of town, you'll find Te Puia, originally the site of a Maori fortress and, today, home to Maori schools for woodcarving and weaving, as well as a traditional meeting house. The Maori built their impregnable fortress here on top of a "hot spot" and have been using the heat for comfort and cooking for hundreds of years.

The geothermal park comprises about 150 acres of bubbling, hissing, steaming, sulfuric materials emerging from the ground. You can count 500 pools. There are boiling mudpots looking chocolate-y, but you wouldn't want to fall into one. It's the kind of place where a mob boss could easily dispose of an inconvenient body.

Sixty-five geyser vents have been identified and seven of them are reliably active. In fact, Pohutu Geyser erupts about twenty times every day in a magnificent burst, shooting dramatically skyward up to about one hundred feet.

Boardwalks will take you up and down and through the gently rolling landscape, accented by hissing steam vents...which brings us to lunch—a steambox lunch.

Plan your visit for around 11 am. Before you head out into the steam vent hinterland, head for the dining room to order your steambox lunch, comprising traditional elements of Maori cooking.

While you marvel at the geysers, mudpots, and sulfuric pools, local cooks will prepare your lunch, seal it, wrap it, and place it in a special "steambox" before lowering it into the ground above a hissing steam vent. The earth does its work and by the time you return, your lunch will be ready; don't forget to watch while the "chefs" haul your steambox lunch out of the ground.

It's boiling hot, of course, so great care is taken at this point. Gingerly, the "chefs" open the box, unwrap the food and present your "home-cooked" steambox lunch to you. The Maori traditional foods are not comparable to a fast-food restaurant, so don't expect a hamburger and French fries. Instead, recognize that you are there to sample food that is representative of the local indigenous culture. Bon appetit!

I recommend a local Sauvignon Blanc (not included) to accompany this unique lunch, but with or without, it's a remarkable demonstration of a traditional way of life. Who needs electricity?

PERU

AWANACANCHA
IQUITOS
MACHU PICCHU

LLAMA ENCOUNTER & FEEDING

Machu Picchu sits at 8,000 feet, high in the Andes mountains of Peru, and visitors to the Inca citadel will need to complete several legs of a journey to get there. Lima, the capital, hosts the big international airport through which most travelers arrive. From Lima, a flight will bring you to Cuzco, the historic Imperial City. From Cuzco, you can take a train directly to Aguas Calientes, the town at the base of Machu Picchu. But the wise traveler heads to Rio Sagrado (the Sacred Valley) for a few days first. From Rio Sagrado, a train will finish the journey from Ollantaytambo to Aguas Calientes.

Rio Sagrado offers five-star hotels in a gorgeous setting. Local activities include touring the Inca town at Pisac, the old Inca fortress at Ollantaytambo, and the wonderful Moray Salt Pans. Importantly, a few days' sojourn here allows your body to acclimate to the elevation so that your visit to Machu Picchu is less likely to bring on altitude sickness.

When you drive from Cuzco to Rio Sagrado, plan to stop at the little Awanacancha Textile center on the way. Can you picture the vivid colors that define the native Peruvians' clothing? Bright pinks, oranges, greens, blues, purples, yellows—the local women use all these glorious colors as they weave their traditional costumes. Awanacancha can show you how it all happens.

At the Awanacancha textile center, fourteen local communities focus on the weaving traditions passed down for centuries. This private project helps preserve the art of Andean weavings and provides economic assistance to the local people.

In Europe and North America, we think of wool as a product of sheep farming. In the Andes mountains, wool comes off the backs of llamas, vicunas, alpacas, and their various cousins. These animals all comprise "camelid" beasts and they roam freely in their warm coats through the high mountain altitudes. Occasionally, they allow humans to take the wool off their bodies and make it into clothing. The llamas and alpacas and vicunas are very accommodating that way.

Naturally, a textile center needs wool on hand, and so a small herd of alpacas and llamas live at Awanacancha. While these friendly beasts loll about in a small enclosure, they happily munch on the grassy stalks that you can pick up and share with them. They also graciously pose for pictures. They like to stand very close and once they see you have food for them, they will come right up to you and take it from your hand. Snap. Post on Facebook or Instagram.

Once you've finished feeding a llama or two or three, head inside to watch women at their work of weaving. They usually dress in their traditional outfits. You will see that their life in the mountains requires warm clothing. As their skillful hands click in and out of the textiles in progress, you can sense the oral traditions and knowledge that have passed from generation to generation.

In a separate area, a broad array of plants and insects demonstrate how the local people use the nature around them to create the vivid colors of yarn so typical of the region. Although modern factories in the cities use automation and synthetic dyes, here in the mountains, color derives from what lies at hand.

For red, the women first dry a small insect called a cochineal before grinding it into a fine powder with a mortar and pestle. Adding certain fixatives in the dying process also allows weavers to create fuschia, pinks, and purples, as well as true red.

For orange, the bark of *yanali*, a local tree found in high altitudes gets chopped into small pieces and then boiled. *Yanali* results in a mustard yellow or yellowish-orange color. For a brighter orange, *qaqa sunkha* is boiled with the yarn.

Green generally derives from *ch'illca*, a leafy green plant with white flowers. Large bunches of fresh leaves can be mixed with *collpa*, a mineral from the local jungle, before boiling. *Collpa* is also added to a local pod called *tara* to get different shades of green. Depending on how long dyes are boiled, blues can range from royal blue to grey.

After dyeing has achieved the desired intensity of color, fixatives such as mineral salts or urine allow for setting a color or intensifying color saturation. Once the desired color has set, the weavers rinse the wool and dry it before using.

Awanacancha occupies a small space in the universe of Peru and the Machu Picchu tourist business. A stop here doesn't take very long but will absolutely impart a sense of Andean life as it has been lived before, during, and after the Incas and the Spanish conquistadors.

HEADWATERS OF THE AMAZON

The incredible citadel of Machu Picchu sits near the top of many people's bucket list, and with good reason. The Lost City of the Incas lends itself to mystery, primitivism, history, and a little Indiana Jones.

To get there and back from Lima via Cuzco and the Sacred Valley generally requires about six days to do properly. That's a little short for a bucket list vacation; why not enhance your trip to Peru with a few days in the Amazon?

The legendary 2,300-mile Amazon River begins deep in the Peruvian jungle where the Pacaya and the Ucayali Rivers meet, forming the Pacaya Samiria National Reserve in the middle.

A two-hour flight from Lima will bring you to Iquitos where you will board your twenty-four passenger luxury river boat. Be sure to sit near the window; the view of the river carving its leisurely way through the massive emerald jungle below is mesmerizing. On the other hand, if you look down and think about what lives in that jungle, you might quail just a bit.

Upon arrival in Iquitos, the boat company will take over, starting with transportation to the embarkation point. From now until you disembark, three, four, or seven days later, all of your needs will be handled by the boat crew. Every day, you will board a small "panga" (like an inflatable zodiac) to explore the inlets and rivers of the region with your naturalist, in small groups of six or seven passengers. Generally, the schedule includes two excursions per day with a break for lunch and rest between. Your naturalist guide may well be someone who grew up in the region, but acquired an education, good English skills, and biology training.

Bird lovers will savor every minute in the Pacaya Samiria reserve. Scarlet macaws swoop overhead. The bizarre hanging nests of the oropendola dot the trees. The list goes on and on, but you could certainly spot harpy eagles, toucans, and Amazon kingfishers to name just a few. The rainbow of colors flying through the trees and over the river constantly piques your vision.

In the waters around you and your boat live pink dolphins, caimans, manatees, yellow spotted

144

river turtles and, yes, piranhas. On land, you might see howler and tamarin monkeys, sloths, and the big mammals called capybaras. In short, the jungle teems with life, both flora and fauna right at your fingertips.

Happily, for those of you who feel...well...a bit skittish about reptiles and creepy-crawlies, your boat will keep you safely apart from anything you don't want to get close to. Let's face it: it's much easier to appreciate the beauty and agency of the snakes who live in the jungle if there's water between you and them.

The boat captain usually makes an effort to find a riverside village to visit, but landing depends on water levels, time of year, and safe passage up a riverbank for the passengers. If a landing is possible, the crew will advise you that you won't want to arrive empty handed. In the small store on board, you can purchase a small gift for the villagers: pencils and a notebook for kids, laundry soap and household items for the women, and fishing supplies for the men. Bearing your gift, you will find yourself interacting with river people who might not have seen another visitor for eighteen months. If you plan in advance of your journey, bring items from home, but remember that the riverside dwellers have simple needs and minimal electricity.

Did I mention the nighttime excursion? Here's your chance to see what comes out after dark from the safety of a boat. As the sun sets, your guide will hand you a pole with a long string, already baited with a small piece of meat. You will then go piranha-fishing. You can be sure that you, too, will bring up one of those fearsome critters after you feel that bite on the pole. Up close and personal, your guide will show you all those razor-sharp teeth before release.

After dark, your naturalist guide will point out all the creepy crawlies. Best that they stay on the riverbanks and that you stay on board. Perhaps you'll learn the rule of thumb about how to tell what lies behind that pair of eyes in the bush. Are the eyes blinking? It's a bird. Are they not blinking? It's a snake. Useful to know.

By definition, jungle temperatures stay warm year-round, and the river cruise is available whatever time of year you'd like to visit. However, rainy or dry season does make a difference. In the dry season, your excursion may slice deeper into the jungle due to more available land. During the wet season, the boat will use the high water to roam farther into creeks and flooded byways.

These very comfortable boats offer great food and drink and comfortable cabins. The expeditions include transportation to and from Iquitos, food and drink on board, and all of your daily excursions. This is not an inexpensive tour, but it's worth every penny.

GATE OF THE SUN

Machu Picchu visitors all experience the same thrill when they pass through the admission gate and encounter their first sight of the lost city of the Incas below. That same view graces every Bucket List calendar and travel book, since it captures the vast and mysterious complex perfectly.

Climbing up and down the myriad steps and traversing the flat stones of this mysterious city will take more than a few minutes and, ideally, a good guide will explain what the ruins tell us about the life of the people who built and lived at Machu Picchu. Since the Incas did not use a written language, many mysteries abide to this day. How did these pre-industrial people transport the enormous stones and boulders here? How were the stone walls constructed so perfectly without mortar? Was Machu Picchu a fortress? A religious site? A city for the Inca aristocracy?

One fact is clear: Machu Picchu sits in a perfect position for defense, surely not an accident. High on a mountaintop about eighty miles from the imperial Inca city of Cusco, all visitors to the citadel (or sanctuary) had to travel one path starting from the Urubamba River and traversing the Andes Mountains. This historic Inca trail covers twenty-six miles and reaches elevations of almost 14,000 feet. After a multi-day hike, travelers arrived at *Inti Punku* or Gate of the Sun.

Depending on your fitness level, taste for hard adventure, and possession of a permit, you can hike the Inca Trail today, assisted by a good outfitter. For those short on time and perhaps not quite so ambitious, there's an easier alternative. Make sure you buy two separate entrance tickets to Machu Picchu for successive days. On day one, tour the main site. On day two, come back and hike to the Gate of the Sun.

The well-marked trail departs from the back of the citadel. Rough, broad stones underfoot lead ever upward, as you skirt the edge of the mountain. Most of the path lies on a gentle incline, but it alternately dips and rises. You do need to watch your step, lest you twist an ankle. Railings border parts of the path, but not all of them. In several spots, the path is quite narrow, and you may meet other trekkers coming from the opposite direction. Someone might need to give way and wait for the oncoming walker to pass before proceeding onward. Remember, you're walking along the side of a mountain. Pay attention to what you're doing.

The hike takes about ninety minutes and you can savor stunning views of the lush, jade-green Andes mountains, valleys, and peaks all around you. You'll find plenty of places to stop, rest, and take pictures along the way. Notably, the path does not afford views of the citadel since you are heading away from it.

Once you arrive at the Gate of the Sun, you'll find a pleasant spot to rest, relax, and channel your inner Inca, reflecting on the mysteries of the past. You can also marvel at the incredibly fit hikers coming off the Inca Trail to arrive at Machu Picchu. Invariably, they are young, strong, and bubbling over with energy. The walk down is easier and faster for everyone.

Note: *Alternatively with that second day of admission to Machu Picchu, you can choose to climb Huayna Picchu (the adjacent mountain) or to walk over to see the Inca Bridge, a marvel of primitive construction in its own right.*

SCOTLAND

THE HIGHLANDS
STIRLING

HIGHLAND GAMES

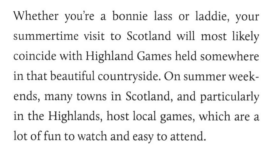

Whether you're a bonnie lass or laddie, your summertime visit to Scotland will most likely coincide with Highland Games held somewhere in that beautiful countryside. On summer weekends, many towns in Scotland, and particularly in the Highlands, host local games, which are a lot of fun to watch and easy to attend.

The Highland Games tradition dates back hundreds of years. King Malcolm III summoned men to race up Craig Choinnich overlooking Braemar with the aim of finding the fastest runner in Scotland to be his royal messenger. That was in sometime between 1031 and 1093!

The early Games also provided an opportunity for the strongest and bravest soldiers to demonstrate their strength and bravery. At the same time, musicians and dancers were encouraged to attend and show off their talents for the glory of the local Scottish clans. The Games in Fife hold bragging rights as the oldest continuously held competition, dating back to 1314.

Today's contests clearly hark back to those origins. A Highland Games competition usually begins with a gathering of locals in the center of town in the morning. Some of the towns are quite small, and you might find just a hundred people gathering in the main square. The locals of both genders and all ages often wear kilts, kicking off the day with a parade through the streets, eventually ending at the field of competition.

During the competition, you'll see brawny (and I mean BRAWNY) men in kilts and t-shirts compete in feats of strength. The Scottish Hammer Throw requires tossing a very heavy hammer up over a high bar. A stone put tests how far you can throw...you guessed it...a stone. Tossing other heavy items in the air also makes up part of the competition.

Foot races intersperse the heavy object-throwing. There are long distance races. There are short distance races. There are intermediate distance races. Some of the racers may compete barefoot, even as they vanish over the hills to return to the main field for the final leg. Over the course of several hours, you will probably see that one or two competitors will best almost everyone else. Athletic prowess dominates, but remember: the contenders wear kilts, not running shorts.

Everyone's favorite sport has to be the caber toss. Picture a long telephone pole; picture a very substantial guy in a kilt. He will pick up the caber by one end, with a great deal of grunting and struggle. He will somehow manage to hoist the thing up in the air by himself and then throw it forward, end to end, as far as he can. The idea is to heave the caber as far as possible, keeping it close to the 12 o'clock position. It's hard to imagine just why an ancient king would want a soldier to do that specific task, but there must have been a reason. It's also hard to imagine these beefy guys practicing this year after year in the modern world so that they can win.

In keeping with the historical tradition, bagpiping and Highland dance competitions usually accompany the games. For true aficionados of bagpiping, a preliminary competition might occur the night before the games. Whether you savor all bagpiping all the time or not, during the Games, the pipers will periodically appear on the sidelines to breathe and squeeze those Scottish bags. It might be hard for an amateur visitor to discern the fine differences in skill and emotion between the players, but the music is gorgeous and evocative.

Highland dancers will also compete for prizes on the sidelines, even as the games proceed on the field. The dancers are usually teenagers, and these ladies and gents will delicately and precisely dance intricate patterns of steps over crossed swords. The traditional outfits and fresh faces make for a lovely spectacle.

You can check the schedule of Highland Games online at the Scottish Highland Games Association website (https://www.rshga.org). You'll see that they are well-organized and distributed throughout Scotland, running from April to early September. With approximately one hundred Highland Games to choose from, it's pretty easy to line up your vacation with an event. You can buy tickets online in advance, and it's helpful to spend the night in the town where the games will occur.

WILLIAM WALLACE MONUMENT

Aye, ye fans of legendary Scottish heroes. Put on your strongest Scottish brogue and head northwest from Edinburgh to Stirling, site of the famous castle that controlled access to the Highlands and, thus, controlled the country back in warrior days. While Stirling Castle definitely merits a visit, since you're in the neighborhood, seek out the nearby monument to William Wallace of *Braveheart* fame.

Formally known as the Wallace National Monument, this striking tower sits atop the Abbey Craig, a rocky outcropping that Wallace used as his headquarters before the Battle of Stirling Bridge in 1297. You'll need to climb 246 steps to ascend the viewing platform, which commands a fine view of the surrounding countryside. You'll enjoy a panorama stretching from Ben Lomond and the Trossachs in the west, and through the Forth Valley past the city of Stirling and the Ochil Hills to the Pentland Hills in the east.

Naturally, having a fine view of the surrounding countryside meant something different to Wallace than it does to you, the modern visitor. Just before the big battle, Wallace reportedly watched the army of King Edward I of England gather. Inside the monument, you'll find several items on display including the Wallace Sword, a five-foot, four-inch long sword weighing almost seven pounds. That should give you a good sense of what kind of fighting Wallace expected.

The Scottish Wars of Independence were raging at the time of the famous battle. The English had imposed control over the region under King Edward I, and the local Scots rose up to oppose it. Although vastly outnumbered, their strategies were effective, and the English soldiers sustained heavy losses. Although the events depicted in the film *Braveheart* blend local lore from other nearby battles, the setting and the story made for a stirring film.

When you ascend the tower, look for a Scots soldier attired in medieval garb standing guard. Of course, these friendly warriors will happily explain what they're wearing and whose army they belong to. More important, they can and want to share fantastic and dramatic stories of brave Scots warriors who fought for their country. If you're interested in hearing these tales of bravery, treachery, conquest, and more, you just have to ask.

Spoiler alert: These Scottish soldiers are really actors underneath their armor. That makes them particularly good storytellers, and Scotland's tempestuous and bloody history provides unending drama. With an eager audience of even one person, they will relate tale after tale after tale.

Recommendation: ask for the story of the famous Scottish king Robert the Bruce, the battle of Bannockburn, and the Battle Axe. Ignore everything you thought you learned from *Braveheart*. You can visit the National Wallace Monument website (nationalwallacemonument.com) to find out when you're likely to get the maximum theatrical experience.

SLOVENIA

LJUBLJANA

STAND UP PADDLE

Want to escape the crowds thronging the space in front of the *Mona Lisa*? Can't handle the "rush hour" traffic in the pedestrian zone of Dubrovnik? Need a break from the three-hour line to enter the Vatican museum?

Yes, you can still find quiet corners of Europe if you stray off the beaten track. Can you imagine propelling yourself on a stand up paddleboard (SUP) through the heart of a country's capital city?

Slovenia, a small country to the east of Italy and south of Austria, boasts a charming and picturesque capital, Ljubljana, a city of less than 300,000 people. Nestled in the Julian Alps, the country draws on strong cultural influences from its better-known neighbors. As a result, Ljubljana presents tidy and colorful baroque buildings, offset with a more modern art deco vibe as a result of earthquake damage in 1895.

As a European capital, it sits in the shadow of the requisite castle on the hill. Red tiled roofs dot the skyline, and monuments and obelisks punctuate the town squares. Bridges and fountains contain countless little flourishes, and right in the center of it all flows the gentle, emerald green Ljubljanica river.

Ljubljana's history dates to Roman times and, according to legend, even further. Supposedly, Jason (as in Jason and the Argonauts) returned here after winning the golden fleece and slew a monster in the swamp of the present-day city.

Although the city's profile has risen in recent years, it still offers opportunities for discovery at a gentler pace than other European capitals. Can you imagine trying to pilot a stand-up paddleboard down the traffic-heavy Grand Canal of Venice? (You'd be run over by the *vaporetto* or even a gondola within a few minutes.) How about down the Seine in the heart of Paris? Too many Bateaux Mouches and their happy passengers on every side. Around lower Manhattan where the Hudson opens into the harbor of New York City? Fugeddaboutit! Dodging the Staten Island Ferry, the tugboats and barges, and even the Queen Mary 2 at times would take a few years off your life.

But Ljubljana says, why not? They've got plenty of room and it's not that busy. Even if you've never tried SUP before, you can do it. The river does not get much traffic and the water is calm. The boards are stable, and you can practice by kneeling at first before you haul yourself up to your full *homo erectus* position.

Seeing any city or site from the water always adds a wonderful and new perspective. Most major cities began as ports along a river, so the view from the water harkens back to an earlier age. Ljubljana is no different. You'll find yourself floating down a tranquil waterway at a human pace. Periodically, you'll pass under iconic bridges while envious tourists gaze down at you. Cafés and pretty buildings dot the riverbanks; feel free to wave at the patrons shoreside.

Most of the SUP tours last about two hours. Although SUP does not require a lot of expertise to get started, two hours will give you a pleasant workout and perhaps more, if you're a novice. You can usually dip into the river at the end of the tour if you're so inclined, weather permitting.

Note: *Swimming ability is required for obvious reasons.*

SOUTH AFRICA

PHINDA

RHINO ENCOUNTER

On the northeastern coast of South Africa lies the private Phinda Private Game Reserve, 70,560 acres of protected wildlife land in KwaZulu-Natal. Here, you'll find the Big Five (lion, leopard, elephant, buffalo, and rhino), as well as 436 bird species happily sharing woodland, grassland, wetland, and forest. The reserve is particularly well known for close-up sightings of the elegant yet elusive cheetah, as well as the rare black rhino.

The rhinoceri are well tended and cared for within the park, with a commitment to sustaining a healthy population. Veterinary teams monitor the population closely for research and security through periodic ear notching. Ear notches allow researchers to correctly identify individual rhinos. And while they're at it, the vets measure the animals, collect skin samples, and shave the horns for DNA analysis.

Many of Phinda's rhinos are in need of ear notches, and you can participate!

This experience begins with the veterinary team taking to the skies in a helicopter in search of rhinos. On the ground, a visitor can follow in hot pursuit with an expert ranger in an open 4x4 safari vehicle, holding up to eight people.

From the air, a team targets a rhinoceros. The vet shoots a tranquilizer dart at the animal from the helicopter and waits for the anesthesia to take effect. Then, the helicopter lands, the vets alight and signal that the visitors on the ground can approach safely. Now, you—the visitor—will have the never-to-be-repeated opportunity to touch the anaesthetized rhino during the notching procedure.

These fearsome beasts continually amaze us humans by their very appearance. Everyone from Rudyard Kipling in *Just So Stories* to a child of five at the zoo can only marvel at the baggy, leathery skin, the oversized and graceless body, and that horn, that very sharp horn.

The skin itself can be up to two inches thick as it lies in those overlapping folds. And yet, a rhino is subject to sunburn, which is why you'll often see a rhino rolling in the mud. Once the mud dries, it provides protection from both the sun and from insects.

Those massive bodies can weigh up to 5,000 pounds, making rhinos the biggest land animals after elephants. A rhino can reach six feet high and eleven feet long.

In spite of a chunky body, a rhinoceros can run up to thirty miles per hour. At top speed, rhinos gallop on their toes. Don't try to outrun one; they'll beat your top speed of twenty-eight miles per hour. Luckily for you, their eyesight is quite poor, so you might be able to serpentine your way to safety. Unluckily for you, their acute sense of smell may help them run you down in spite of your elusive measures.

How does a rhino that is not asleep communicate with other animals, including humans? They like to snort, which is never a good sign for any species. That means an angry animal. If a rhino huffs at you, they may be just saying, "hi." A surprised squeak? "I'm confused." And you thought they didn't have much to say!

One of the surprising aspects of an "up close and personal encounter" with a sleeping rhinoceros is the discovery that the rhino's horn is actually made of keratin (like our fingernails) based on hair, densely packed hair. While your favorite rhino dozes away, you can touch that horn and marvel that hair can be made into such a fearsome weapon!

Humans have an instinctive respect for these bizarrely shaped beasts, and well we should. They don't much like humans or anyone besides other rhinos. Their fearsome mass and that very serious horn are not things to take lightly.

If you can pet a rhino while it's sleeping and know that the veterinary team is helping it survive and thrive in the Phinda game reserve, do it! Any fees you pay will go to the conservation efforts in the Reserve, making your outing a win-win for man and beast.

SPAIN

GUIJUELO

SALAMANCA

TARRAGONA, MÉRIDA, SEVILLE

HAM TASTING

Vegetarians—Please turn the page.

Although the rain in Spain falls mainly on the plain, there's a great reason to head north of Madrid into Castile, where the legends of Don Quixote and the medieval warrior El Cid are alive and well. Cities like Salamanca, Leon, and Ávila draw tourists and with good reason. But YOU are looking for pigs; yes, pigs.

Near Salamanca lies the small town of Guijuelo and the Alma de Ibérico showroom; we're talking Spanish ham. Many of us appreciate Spanish ham as among the best in the world, but it can be difficult to find in the US. Spanish exporters have to contend with labyrinthine USDA regulations in order to enter the US market, and most of them don't bother. Thus, Spanish ham enthusiasts should go directly to Spain.

At the Alma de Ibérico showroom, you will enter a simple, well-lit tasting room outfitted with a carving station, simple barrel tables and seats for spectators, and a small display area with products for sale. Look up to see a forest of myriad and savory cured Spanish hams suspended from the ceiling and waiting for eager palates.

While you perch around a table, the *jamonista* (apologies to Starbucks) emerges from the back with a virgin ham leg. Whether young or old, this master carver has developed finely honed carving skills. He begins slowly and delicately, and his activity looks deceptively easy. A small slice. Then another. And another.

While you watch, he fills a plate with rosettes of luscious ham, artistically arranged on a large plate to resemble a flower. A server brings the plate to you; it is a feast for your eyes.

The carver continues to carve. Another plate of rosettes materializes. The server brings the plate to another guest. Now, sighs of appreciation begin to bubble up from each barrel table. And still the carver carves on.

Your server will offer you wine to whet your palate and enhance the experience of tasting, rating, and enjoying the results of the master carver at work . While your senses savor the taste, the beauty, the feel, and the aromas at your table, the *jamonista* carves on, creating plate after plate of ham rosettes to be distributed among the happy tasters.

Perhaps you'd care to try a little fresh sausage? Some chorizo? Shall you add a little cheese? Say yes, and these items appear. Finally, when you cannot eat one more slice of anything, a small dessert magically appears at your table. The sweetness of the small tart complements the savory, and somehow, you can eat just a little bit more.

And now the question: Who would like to try their skill at carving? "Oh, that doesn't look that hard," you think. After all, don't I carve a turkey every November? You pick up the knife and slice. The slice is thick. It looks nothing like a rosette. You try again. You produce a slice slightly thinner, but not much. Again, no rosette appears. A couple of more tries will convince you that you have a lot to learn about this particular and delicate skill.

Instead, the wiser course is to buy Spanish ham to bring home with you. While you are finishing up, the friendly proprietors add to your knowledge.

Q. What makes this ham so delicious?
A. The local pigs range free and dine on only grass.

Q. Does it make a difference to the quality of the ham whether it comes from a right or a left leg?
A. No. A legend has grown up that the pigs lean more on one leg, making the other leg more tender. Nope: pigs lean on both legs equally.

Be sure to pick up the business card as you leave. This Spanish ham producer DOES sell its products in the United States.

WILL YOU BE A REPROBATE AT SALAMANCA UNIVERSITY?

Salamanca, north of Madrid in Spain, boasts one of the four oldest continuously operating universities in Europe. Guess the other three. Give up? Oxford, Bologna, and Padua. The Sorbonne in Paris? *Mais, non.* The Sorbonne shut down for a bit during the French Revolution, thus not continuously operating.

The University of Salamanca was established in 1134 and is considered the most prestigious school in Spain today. The city is even older, dating back to the Roman era. In fact, an old Roman bridge, replete with classical arches, still spans the Tormes River.

Salamanca itself differs from many European cities in that its historical attractions don't have much to do with churches. Of course, the university originated as a cathedral school, but your visit here is less about exploring a cathedral or a church with Renaissance art and more about learning the stories of the university's early days. And they are fascinating!

One of the first things you will learn is that you must search for the frog hidden on the facade of the university's main building. You will join an enthusiastic crowd, standing in the plaza, staring at the intricate carvings over La Puerta de Salamanca. Every now and then, an enthusiastic "Aha!" rings out.

After you've finished the frog hunt, head into the old university buildings where the hard facts of university life in the twelfth century emerge. Your high school Latin will come in handy as you read the plaques over the various rooms.

Be sure to visit the stunning early library with its evocative wooden tiers of books arranged around a lovely open atrium. The burnished wood fixtures, the historic books, and the handwritten classifications of "knowledge" in the 1200s look nothing like your average suburban library of today. Think of the thousands of students who have acquired knowledge in these hallowed halls over the generations.

And speaking of acquiring knowledge, some of the facts of early student life are arresting. You can visit a classroom, set up in the traditional fashion. Does it seem a little dark? There are no lights, in fact, because Thomas Edison wouldn't be born for another six hundred years. So, learning took place during daylight hours only.

Note the "pulpit" where the official repeater echoed the words of the professor—which were all in Latin, of course. No one was writing anything down or consulting books. Gutenberg hadn't printed his Bible yet. Students were expected to remember the professor's lesson as "told" to them and then repeated by the assistant for one extra iteration.

And finally, you come to the examination room. It's an elegant room, but one full of angst. On one end of a long table sat the professors who would examine the candidate. The poor trembling student took his turn at the other end, in the examination chair. There were (still are) stone placements for his nervous feet underneath the giant table. Armrests for his twitching limbs. The examination took several hours and, of course, it was in Latin.

After consulting, the august professors might congratulate the diligent student on his accomplishment. The years of study, recitation, and regurgitation of information had paid off. Honor was due.

But pity the poor student who did not pass. He was termed a "reprobate," from the Latin for *provare* (to try, to prove). There was a side door for an exit to which the reprobate was directed for his walk of shame. Slinking outside, he might encounter an unsympathetic crowd jeering and laughing. They were known to pelt the reprobates with rotten vegetables and fruit to drive home their contempt. It was a tough crowd.

Today's students have an easier time. There are lights. There are not only pens and paper, but laptops and tablets. No one sits in that brutal chair, and I do not believe that failure is greeted with rotten fruit anymore—or at least not very often.

By all means, sit in the examinee's chair, grip the armrests, put your feet on the supports, and channel your scholar's graduation test. Failure means that you will henceforth be a "reprobate." What a shame!

On a lighter note, Salamanca is a lively university town and the students' energy is palpable everywhere. On a Saturday in good weather, you'll see groups of young people celebrating an upcoming friends' wedding with bachelor and bachelorette parties. The party members are usually dressed in themed costumes, roaming through the downtown streets, and especially gravitating to the gorgeous Plaza Mayor.

Enjoy the city and give thanks that even if you ARE a reprobate, at least no one is throwing rotten vegetables at you.

ROMAN RUINS

The ancient Romans loved the Iberian Peninsula (modern day Spain and Portugal). They arrived in the late BCE., subdued the local tribes in 206 BC and stayed for almost seven hundred years. They enjoyed the climate, they thought the women were pretty, and the locals submitted without too much trouble. Importantly, they reaped significant economic benefits from their colonies here, which produced plenty of gold, wool, olive oil, and wine for shipping back home. What's not to like?

In exchange for peace and the aforementioned exports, the Romans behaved in a typically Roman fashion and built all the accoutrements needed for their idea of a "modern" society. They administered Iberia through local districts, each with its own headquarters and leaving behind cities such as Zaragoza, Mérida, Valencia, and Tarragona. They constructed excellent roads, arenas for the gory entertainment of their day, bridges and magnificent aqueducts with rows of arches, theaters and libraries, and of course elegant villas with intricate mosaic floors for the local nabobs.

All good things must come to an end, though, and eventually the Romans withdrew as their empire contracted and eventually collapsed. However, their ancient monuments have survived very well in the hot, dry climate of Spain. For Roman history enthusiasts, Spain boasts myriad and well-preserved relics of the ancient era. Better yet, the tourist crowds that throng the Pantheon and the Colosseum in Rome are nowhere to be seen in Spain.

Tarragona lies an easy hour south of Barcelona by local train. This seaside town boasts a well-preserved arena, the remains of a larger "circus" complex, and an archaeological museum, heavy on the Roman era with some beautiful mosaics. Admittedly, the museum is a tad dusty and in need of an update, but between the arena and the museum, a Roman-ruins enthusiast can spend a pleasant day here. You'll find palm trees dotting the local landscape in the Mediterranean climate and a terrace overlooking the arena and sea beyond it. If by chance you've traveled by car, you can find an impressive aqueduct, known locally as the Devil's Bridge (Pont del Diablo) about five miles outside of town and a triumphal arch a few miles further on.

Further south in the heart of Andalusia lies the lively university town of Seville. Although it's a major tourist attraction today, its origins date back all the way to the Punic Wars between Rome and Carthage. After all, Spain lies just across the Straits of Gibraltar from Africa and Carthage (modern Tunisia). One of the conquering heroes of the Second (of three) Punic War was Scipio Africanus. As a caring and thoughtful general, he sought to create a haven for his troops returning from the second war with Carthage—the one with Hannibal and the elephants. He called it Italica, and you'll find it about nine kilometers outside of Seville.

Very few visitors make their way to Italica, but the arena there remains in excellent condition. It originally held about 25,500 spectators and was the third largest in the Roman Empire at the time of its construction. On a quiet fall morning, you might find yourself among the whistling winds, sitting in the spectator seats, with not another person in sight. For those seeking to channel the ancient spirits, Italica provides extremely favorable circumstances.

Nearby, you can also find the remains of several old houses with beautiful mosaics, still visible, a little bit of an ancient aqueduct, and skeletal ruins of a Roman theater.

In the west of Spain, the Romans needed an administrative center, and they founded one at Mérida, in the wild and sparsely populated region near the border with Portugal known as Estremadura. This small town boasts a dual identity. It happened to produce several conquistadors famous for their sailing and conquering exploits. You'll notice the streets named for Pizzaro and Cortez as you wander about.

Mérida has preserved its Roman identity even better. In fact, you'll find more Roman ruins here than anywhere else in Spain. Look for the Temple of Diana, the beautiful two-story facade of the ancient theater, the Arch of Trajan, the amphitheater, and the remains of the Circus, designed for chariot racing.

The facade of the theater is particularly impressive. And, naturally, you'll spot an aqueduct nearby with classic Roman arches. The city has also built a first-rate museum of Roman antiquities with some beautiful mosaic floors to appreciate.

HUMAN PYRAMID

You'll find Catalonia in the northeast corner of Spain, bounded by the Pyrenees Mountains, boasting its own language (Catalan) and traditions, and celebrating a long separatist history. The wild and rugged coast (the Costa Brava) shields an interior full of mountains and hills.

The vibrant city of Barcelona gets lots of visitors these days in a renaissance that many date to the Olympic Games of 1992. It has transitioned from a faded and dusty port to a city evincing the bizarre architecture of Antonio Gaudi, a lusty food and wine culture, Roman origins, and internationally renowned museums of Pablo Picasso and Joan Miro.

But wait, there's more. South of Barcelona lies another town with Roman origins and a good archaeological museum, Tarragona. Here a festival every other year in October showcases *castells* or human pyramids. In this competition, the *castell* teams vie for the honor of building the tallest structure, made entirely out of people. The competition uses a vast arena that can hold as many eighty-five separate teams. And YOU can attend.

This unique tradition reaches back to the 1700s, deriving from the Valencian Dance of southern Spain, *Bal des Valencians*. Within the last fifty years, the tradition has spread throughout Catalonia, evolving into a modern spectacle. Although originally all-male, women have participated since the 1980s, leading to lighter and stronger *castells* that can reach nine or even ten "stories."

More than four hundred people usually engage in the construction and support of a *castell*. The distinct phases begin at the bottom in a crush of brave and dedicated souls. These hardy individuals provide the "platform" that will support the pyramid as it soars ever higher. The pressure on the bodies at the bottom can lead to fainting and injury.

Once the *pinya* (the base of the tower) forms, the climbers who will make upper layers move to a position for easy access to their places in the tower. As subsequent base levels are completed, the *castellers* in the *pinya* constantly assess if the base is solid enough for construction to continue. If it is, climbers go up and form still higher levels.

Finally, at a signal, bands begin to play the traditional Toc de Castells music as a hush comes over spectators. The upper layers of the tower are built as quickly as possible to minimize strain on the lower *castellers* who bear most of the weight. At last, a small (and very light) four- or five-year-old child climbs up nine levels of people and stands up proudly. (Yes, they wear helmets.) At the top, this ultimate climber (the *enxaneta)* raises one open hand to signal that the *castell* is complete!

The disassembly of the *castell*, done amidst the cheering of the crowd, is often the most treacherous stage of the event. First, the *enxaneta* descends the opposite side of the tower, after which subsequent layers begin to move down, carefully and methodically, until, finally, the *pinya* is "released" and can break apart. The watchwords for a *castell* team are: Strength. Balance. Courage. Common Sense.

The climbers are usually barefoot both for traction and to avoid injury to the support layers. The teams sport colorful costumes, making a gorgeous human landscape in the arena. Typically, *castellers* wear white trousers, a black sash (*faixa*), a bandana (*mocador*), and their team shirt with the team emblem.

The *faixa* represents the tradition as a whole and is only worn during the construction of a *castell*. The sash may provide additional support to the lower back, but importantly, other *castellers* can use the sash as foothold or handhold when climbing up the tower. The higher the climber, the shorter the sash.

Some teams win year after year, but all teams must practice extensively to have a chance at both successfully completing the *castell* and gaining the title. Not all *castells* are successfully completed, and there is precise terminology to describe how far a *castell* got in a given competition.

- *Descarregat*: The tower is completed to the top—that is, to the point where the enxaneta raises his or her hand in the *aleta* gesture—and successfully dismantled.
- *Carregat*: The tower is completed to the top but falls during dismantling.
- *Intent*: The tower falls before it is completed.
- *Intent desmuntat*: The tower is not completed to the top but is successfully dismantled because the tower is unstable and likely to fall.

Surprisingly, perhaps due to common sense, serious injuries are uncommon.

Tarragona highlights this wonderful tradition with a day of live music, dance performances, local talent, and sometimes fireworks to celebrate the completion of the towers. If you can't make it to Tarragona in October for the competition every other year, a Museum of Castells in Valls is under construction.

ST. MAARTEN

PHILIPSBURG

THE SUNSET CAFÉ

What do you get when you mix an active airport runway, a beach, and a Caribbean eatery? The Sunset Café in St. Maarten. This modest little restaurant sits adjacent to the busy airport runway on this lovely island in the sun.

St. Maarten is half-Dutch and half-French, and the island attracts snowbirds from the United States as well as vacationers from the Netherlands and France, all of whom can use direct flights to the island. It's a busy airport, especially during the high season. And if you're an aviation enthusiast or if you simply like very large and loud machines roaring by, read on!

With limited space for a runway big enough to handle standard international jet traffic, St. Maarten constructed its landing strip directly beyond a ten-foot strip of sand that comprises a "vest-pocket" and popular beach. The runway is right at sea level and only a two-lane road separates the beginning of the runway and the beach. Since man and machine are destined to inhabit the same limited space, the authorities have constructed a chain link fence to keep people off the runway—a sensible idea. But that doesn't mean that airplane lovers and thrill seekers of all shapes and sizes can't congregate on the beach.

Picture a steady stream of large jets, small private planes, and everything in-between forming a regular channel of arrivals all morning long. The landing pattern calls for all pilots to approach in a straight line over the sea, lowering altitude until touchdown occurs just a few feet after land begins. All pilots handle their touchdowns slightly differently, which means that some of those jets land a third of the way down the runway and some of them land almost at the beginning.

For a plane touching down near the start of the runway, the altitude of that plane over the people on the beach or on the road or even clinging to the chain link fence is extremely low. The belly of the fuselage might be no more than fifteen feet above the heads of the people on land. Even those that land further down the runway are still pretty darn low over the beach. Those planes are big, they are noisy, they are made of metal, and they are overwhelming to mere humans at close range.

Dangerous, you think? Can be. In the afternoon, the stream of jets reverses as passengers sadly leave their Caribbean beach vacations to head home to their normal lives. At that time, the line forms for planes waiting to take off. This is a one-way runway and take-off occurs in the same direction as landing.

The practical effect of take-off is an enormous backwash of air from the jet engines that have to lift those planes off the ground in a very short space. The far end of the runway faces some hills, so there is not much room for error on take-off. Gentlemen: start your engines! Full power as soon as possible is required.

People positioned on the beach or clinging to the chain link fence have been blown backwards into the water as the jet engines rev. Numerous videos of the landings and take-offs at the St. Maarten beach are available on YouTube, showing these sequences routinely.

Probably the most dramatic video involves a KLM 747 approaching the runway. That's a monster of a plane, and you can see the people on the beach are pretty impressed by the events overhead. Sadly, KLM (now owned by Air France) no longer uses the 747 for St. Maarten, and beach observers must be content with Boeing 737s and Airbus 300s.

For a safer alternative than the beach or the chain-link fence, head to the Sunset Café, sitting safely along one side of the runway. It's still very close to the action, but observers are not directly in the line of fire. Lunch, cocktails, and dinner are all available here, and you will need to patronize the café with food and/or drink to sit at one of their tables. That seems a fair trade for a ringside seat.

You'll find yourself in a happy and enthusiastic crowd with onlookers peering out to sea and trying to be the first one to spot an incoming plane. You can take pictures galore and, of course, videos capture the action even better. Why not wave at some of the arriving passengers in their little windows? You're that close.

If your Caribbean cruise makes a port call at St. Maarten, you can easily hire a taxi to share in the fun. Whether you're on St. Maarten for a day or for a week, if you like planes, really like planes, the airport experience here is for you!

SWEDEN

KIRUNA
ARLANDA AIRPORT

ICE HOTEL

Although it sounds like an urban legend (a very cold urban legend), the Ice Hotel is real, dating back to 1989 and a somewhat fanciful idea. As you can imagine, the Ice Hotel depends on cold temperatures and is thus a seasonal place. You'll find it about 125 miles above the Arctic Circle, a ninety-minute flight from Stockholm.

From December through April each year, a flat space on the banks of the Torne River transforms into a special hotel made of ice and snow. And then the Ice Hotel melts, getting rebuilt the following December. This annual process allows for continual modifications.

The Ice Hotel offers fifteen to twenty standard ice rooms, as well as twelve art suites uniquely designed and hand-carved, all of them created for the very first time.

What's it like to sleep in a room made of ice? You will be toasty. You will be warm. You are meant to feel embraced and protected by the ice, says the creator of the standard ice rooms. Although the room itself keeps a temperature of about 41° F, your bed uses a thick mattress on a wooden base. The bed is covered with reindeer hides, and you will sleep in a thermal sleeping bag. Note: *Instead of doors, the ice rooms have curtains for privacy.*

Are you picturing yourself shivering as you don your PJs and begin reading your novel? It doesn't work that way. Instead, you will change into your PJs in a communal changing room next to the warm lobby, where you'll also find bathrooms and saunas. In other words, your lounging time will occur in a warm place and only your sleeping occurs in the ice room. In the morning, the hotel staff will prepare you a hot lingonberry juice before offering you a session in the sauna and a hot shower. Then, they'll serve you a full breakfast. While you experience your ice night, the hotel will store your luggage securely in the warm lobby area which is open 24/7.

One night in an ice room is probably just about the right amount of time for most of us, and the hotel is well aware of that. Therefore, you'll find traditional and warm rooms onsite as well, so that you can enjoy lots of outdoor and fun activities over a multi-day stay. The Northern Lights, ice sculpture instruction, dog sledding, and snowmobiling expeditions are all at your doorstep. Mush!

JUMBO 747 OVERNIGHT STAY

Do you like planes? REALLY like planes? Do you wish you could sit with the pilots up in the cockpit of that jumbo jet when you fly?

Whether you're a serious aviation enthusiast or simply a traveler seeking inexpensive lodging in a very expensive city, consider the Jumbo Hotel. The Jumbo offers guests an overnight stay in a decommissioned Boeing 747 parked at Stockholm's Arlanda Airport.

In 2009, a local hotelier was looking to add a budget-friendly hotel near the international airport. When he heard that a 1976 Boeing 747 was for sale, he jumped on it and began converting the former Pan Am jet to a modest hostel. After removing all 450 airplane seats, he reconfigured the interior into a series of different room options. Over the years, he's continued to add rooms in places you wouldn't expect.

For your plane trip going nowhere, you can choose a single bunk bed in a four-person, gender-specific "dorm" room. For an "upgrade," choose a standard room in the fuselage featuring a double bed. Note: *Both the dorm rooms and the fuselage bedrooms offer only a shared bathroom experience onboard.*

Interestingly, you can also now head for the wheelhouse rooms, which are built around the wheel assembly and accessed from outside the plane. Or try a "motor" room in one of the old engine cavities, also accessed from outside the plane by a short ladder.

If you are a true aviation enthusiast or you want to splurge, hold out for the Cockpit Double room. Yes, here you can enjoy not only the double bed, but the view out of the cockpit window. You'll find the controls in place and accessible to you, although obviously NOT operational. As the height of luxury on board, the cockpit room also features an ensuite bathroom and shower.

Since all travelers get hungry, the Jumbo Hotel sports a café and simple lounge in the interior of the plane, and alcohol is definitely served on board. You can buy simple snacks, sandwiches, and hot meals to enhance your experience.

What a great opportunity to channel your Capt. Sullenberger and reenact every airplane movie scene you'd like to put yourself into. (You might want to skip *Snakes on a Plane*.)

Because the Jumbo Hotel continually evolves, read on. Perhaps you've marveled at the daredevil wing walkers at airshows? Now, YOU can be one. Yes, with the addition of suitably designed railings, guests can enjoy strolling along the wing and relaxing on its observation deck.

Although it has occupied various locations at the airport since its inception, the Jumbo hotel is now parked permanently near the entrance to the Arlanda complex. And yes, there's a view of the active runways from inside.

Caution: There's no question that the accommodations are much more comfortable than a night spent sitting upright in a coach seat on a transatlantic flight. That all-too-common experience makes us all weary travelers these days. The Jumbo hotel does not offer a luxury experience, but rather a unique one. Welcome aboard!

SWITZERLAND

BAD RAGAZ

ZERMATT

A FONDUE PICNIC IN THE SWISS ALPS

Once upon a time, a German author named Johanna Spyri found herself in the Swiss countryside near Bad Ragaz. She was so inspired by the beauty and simplicity of the Swiss Alps, she wrote a book called *Heidi.* I'm sure you've heard of it; in fact, I'll bet that your image of Switzerland is based on *Heidi.* And indeed, in the hills near Bad Ragaz sits an old wooden hut considered the model for the simple home of Heidi's iconic grandfather.

You'll find the little town of Bad Ragaz southeast of Zurich and just north of Liechtenstein. It's a small and typically Swiss village, famous for its hot springs and its Old World grand hotel and spa. A small river runs through its center with picturesque buildings on each side—perfect for your Swiss photography.

The Swiss are famous for three things: the Alps, chocolate, and fondue. The delicious chocolate and the magnificent Alps are self-explanatory. What about fondue? This staple of Swiss cuisine combines a small pot over a Sterno stove, chunks of bread, and Gruyere cheese. Happily, in

Bad Ragaz you can easily combine the incredible snow-capped mountain scenery of Switzerland with this delicious meal.

In spring, fall, and winter (well, NOT during a blizzard), the Grand Resort Bad Ragaz offers a fondue picnic in a horse-drawn carriage.

You'll meet your driver, carriage, and sturdy and friendly draft horse in front of the hotel. In the warmer months, the carriage is open air. In colder temperatures, Isinglass windows will shield you from the elements while a portable stove keeps you toasty and warm.

Climb in. You'll find two simple benches facing each other across a small wooden table. Red-and-white checked curtains adorn the Isinglass windows, lending a rustic and cheerful ambiance to the outing. Fixed into the center of the table you'll see two fondue pots, just waiting for you to light the Sterno. Your driver will signal the horse to start clip-clopping down the driveway, and you will set off through the streets of this charming town. While the cheese is warming up, feel free to uncork the accompanying bottle of wine. Choose a red or white. They are both locally made.

Soon, you'll leave the town streets behind as you head up into the gentle foothills. By now, your fondue is probably bubbling away with a delicious aroma and enticing look, just begging for you to start dipping while sipping. What's not to like? You've got gorgeous Alpine scenery on every side, simple gastronomic pleasures at hand, and a little liquid something to enhance the whole experience.

Eventually, you'll have mountains in front, in back, and everywhere and, happily, you will even find yourself gazing at vineyards. Yes, the locals can make wine in "Heidi-land," and they do. Mostly you'll find pinot noir for reds and Riesling-Silvaner for whites. Your driver will probably stop in front of the picturesque vineyards for your horse to rest and for you humans to stretch your legs.

Before heading back, your carriage will pass through the tiny little town of Fläsch where Johanna Spyri actually lived while gathering inspiration for her famous book. Afterwards you'll return to Bad Ragaz fed, nurtured, and warm from your Swiss mountainside outing.

FIVE LAKES HIKE

The charming, carless town of Zermatt attracts happy visitors in the depths of winter and in the full bloom of summer. In snow season, skiers flock to the extensive ski runs in the shadow of the iconic Matterhorn. The height of the Alps here means that even in the summer months, a gondola ride up to the Klein Matterhorn might include a few die-hard skiers who will take to the glacier at the top for some off-season "schussing."

The summer months bring alpine flowers, verdant meadows, blue skies, and perfect temperatures to the mountainscape. Even without the skis, a trip to the base of the Klein Matterhorn makes you feel that you are truly at the top of the world. Note that in July and August, it's still pretty cold up there, so dress warmly to mingle among the peaks of the Alps, snow-capped all year long and glistening in the sun under the azure skies. The picture-perfect scenes that you will encounter on every side make you want to breathe deeply, commune with nature, and get out into that landscape.

Zermatt is a small place with one main street. Sometimes a herd of goats or sheep, tended by a small boy, will come right through the center.

It's a great idea to book a stay of at least three nights to have an opportunity to explore the gorgeous mountain scenery all around you. Visitors love taking the gondola up as high as possible; those who are gondola-averse can hop the cog railway up to Gornergrat, the highest train station in Europe. At sea level, the gorge on the edge of town makes for an easy stroll. Since this is Switzerland, the path is in excellent shape with good handrails throughout.

And then, there's the Five Lakes Trail. This is an easy hike of about six miles that passes by five mountain lakes: Stellisee, Grindjisee, Grünsee, Moosjisee, and Leisee. Much of the trail provides good views of the Matterhorn and the world-famous peak is reflected in three of the lakes. Be sure you have at least one camera with you to capture the view. Don't forget to pack a swimsuit if you'd like to jump into the Leisee lake from the small "beach."

From the town, take the funicular up to Sunnegga where you'll change for the gondola to Blauherd and its upper station. At the top, you're ready to set out. The hike itself will probably take about three hours if you walk steadily on the path. But add more time for getting off the trail and following some of the lakeshore paths where possible. And don't worry about getting hungry. There are simple cafes near Lake Grünsee and at Sunnegga where you can buy food or enjoy a sit-down meal if you wish.

The trail is well-marked by yellow signs and you can pick up a free trail map at the funicular station in Zermatt. The path itself varies among gravelly portions and grassy sections. As you pass by the various lakes, you'll want to diverge here and there to explore the small byways and their gorgeous views. Some of the lakes are indeed lake-sized, while at least one of them is more of a pond.

Stellisee, about a one-minute walk from the Blauherd gondola station, is the first lake on the trail. It offers the promised reflection of the Matterhorn and it often gets the vote for "most scenic" of the five lakes.

Grindjisee, the second lake, is much smaller but here, too, the Matterhorn can be seen in its waters. Surrounded by trees and wildflowers, do allot some time to explore the shore path for the best views. You will need to backtrack slightly to the trail afterwards.

Grünsee, the third lake, is set among the starkest of the landscapes, but even there, Swiss pine trees have a found a way to flourish. In addition, wildflowers dot the shore of the lake. The contrast between the rocky land and the green pines is striking. A short walk gives you access to the small mountain lodge, Ze Seewjinu. Outdoor dining on their terrace with views of the Matterhorn is a lovely way to enjoy a midday meal.

After Grünsee, you'll experience a series of switchbacks marked by a waterfall enroute to Moosjisee, the fourth lake. The initial part is uphill, but it will flatten out at a certain point. This is the "pond," notable for its unearthly turquoise color.

Finally, you will arrive at Leisee, the fifth lake. Because the lake offers a small beach and a children's playground, many people congregate here, especially with families. If you didn't swim earlier, you can take an Alpine lake plunge, if you dare. Once you dry off, it's a very short uphill walk to the Sunnegga gondola for your ride back down to Zermatt.

Caution: Skip the alcohol at lunch on this hike. At an altitude of 8,000 feet, alcohol is not your friend. In addition, you'll see that almost all hikers are moving in one direction, as described above. If you start in the opposite direction, the final ascent with switchbacks is demanding.

THAILAND

CHIANG MAI
CHIANG RAI

TUK-TUK ADVENTURE

Even the name *tuk-tuk* sounds exotic. Say it aloud. These three-wheeled, open-air vehicles dot the streets throughout Thailand, from the thronging thoroughfares of urban Bangkok to the quiet country roads in the north. Fares are inexpensive and the ride is jerky, bumpy, and a whole lot of fun. The engines are loud and clearly gas-powered; the name *tuk-tuk* clearly derives from the putt-putt sound of these small motors.

How does a tuk-tuk work? Think of them as a cross between a motorcycle and a small car. A driver sits up front on a bench seat with another bench behind for passengers, and perhaps a small flatbed behind that for transporting goods. A roof shields you from the tropical sun.

The driver uses a clutch and a brake, situated on the floor. The throttle is located near your hands, just like on a motorcycle. If you've never driven a standard transmission vehicle, this adventure is not for you. But if you can drive a stick shift, you can drive a tuk-tuk.

On this full-day adventure, you'll start out at a training area about forty-five minutes outside of Chiang Mai. Here, you'll first accustom yourself to driving the tuk-tuk on a practice area. You'll learn to handle the controls and make sure you're comfortable with the operation of the tuk-tuk. Practice includes driving around a test track and going in and out of traffic cones. Once your instructor is confident that you can do it, it's time to set off.

You and your companions will convoy with a local guide driver in a lead tuk-tuk and another local driver at the rear. Don't worry that you'll have to weave in and out of the famous chaotic Asian traffic scenes. Not so. Your excursion will encompass quiet country roads in the beautiful and quiet Thai countryside. Note: *Tuk-tuks proceed at a slow pace since the motors are quite small.*

Your passengers can enjoy the stunning views as you set off into the lush countryside, pausing for a brief visit at a local traditional temple. A short climb up a hill leads to a great vista of Chiang Mai in the distance. You're likely to be the only tourists in the area and local people may be quite surprised to see non-locals driving tuk-tuks. Don't be shocked that while you're pausing for a picture, someone else is taking a picture of you!

After the stop for the view of Chiang Mai, you'll start to make your way gradually up a small mountain, and your rudimentary driving skills should suffice. You'll have lots of opportunities for photo ops of the gorgeous landscape as you proceed.

Lunchtime will find you at a simple restaurant in the countryside. Afterwards, you will visit a local elephant "home" where the owner will let you meet with and even bathe his friendly pachyderms. This is NOT an opportunity to ride elephants, since modern sensibilities have changed our views of how elephants should be treated.

Once you've had your fill of elephants at rest, enjoy a relaxing float back down a local river before meeting your tuk-tuks again for a return to the starting point. By now, you'll be a confident and experienced tuk-tuk driver, holding your own on these beautiful country roads. Don't worry, you're not expected to drive your tuk-tuk back to Chiang Mai to deal with their traffic!

Tuk-tuks stay in the countryside and you'll catch a ride by minivan back to your hotel in the city.

STROLLING WITH YOUR ELEPHANT

In a remote corner of Southeast Asia, the countries of Thailand, Laos, and Myanmar come together to form the fabled Golden Triangle. Here, a special concerned citizen has created an elephant refuge where you, the enlightened traveler, can interact respectfully with these magnificent creatures.

The refuge at the Anantara Golden Triangle Elephant Camp and Resort is not a breeding station, a zoo, a research facility, or an "elephant ride" tourist attraction. There are plenty of those of varying quality throughout Asia, and we must all be careful to avoid facilities that exploit elephants or treat them cruelly.

Happily, the Elephant Camp and Resort is a place where an elephant owner/handler (*mahout*) is invited to come with his elephant to live. He is offered a job and a place to stay for as long as he wants. He does not sell his elephant, and he and his elephant can leave at any time. However, ideally, he and his elephant change the nature of their lives together by moving here. His elephant can leave behind the horrible circus or the streets of Bangkok or the construction brigade to spend the rest of her life on a grassy plain with appropriate food and care. There is no more work for the elephant, just a life of leisure and recuperation from her previous struggles.

Three times a day, the elephants go for a walk in the forest for exercise. You, the lucky guest at the adjacent hotel, can join them, but, importantly, the exercise takes place routinely whether there are any guests participating or not.

At the day camp, you will meet the *mahouts* and find out about their lives and their work with the elephants. Next, you and the elephants will have a chance to get to know each other. You can touch them and get a sense of their gentleness. You can speak to them and look them in their soulful eyes. You can pat them and nuzzle their ears. You might find that one wraps her trunk around you in your personal encounter.

After your "getting to know you" time, you'll set off for your relaxing stroll together down to the river, with her *mahout* walking alongside her. Along the way, she'll graze on leafy greens and perhaps scratch her back on some convenient bark. The gentle and rhythmic swaying of the walk might even lull you to sleep as you glide along together. Did you know that a Thai expression says that a woman's walk should reflect the grace of an elephant's gait?

Elephants like water, and you will make a stop where you'll see some elephant-sized hoses. Grab one and get ready to play as you dowse your giant friend. It's not clear who gets more pleasure out of the watering: you or the elephant.

Off you go for the final push to the river. When you get there, she's goin' in. She might dunk her head under the water. She might blow water through her trunk, spraying everyone in sight. Repeatedly. Elephants seem to like doing that. When she's had enough water, she'll walk up the embankment and you will make your way back to the base.

When it's time to part, you just might want to hug your huge companion and tell her how much you love her gentle magnificence.

MYANMAR GOLDEN TRIANGLE DAY TRIP

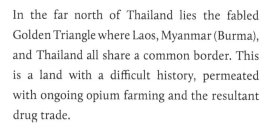

In the far north of Thailand lies the fabled Golden Triangle where Laos, Myanmar (Burma), and Thailand all share a common border. This is a land with a difficult history, permeated with ongoing opium farming and the resultant drug trade.

However, with a private guide and transportation, a casual visit from Chiang Rai, Thailand, to Myanmar is possible and safe for visitors. However, for a multitude of reasons, independent exploration is not recommended. Furthermore, operation of this tour depends on the changing political situation in Myanmar. Be sure to find out in advance if the tour will be possible during your time in Chiang Rai.

The Thai-Myanmar Goodwill Bridge spans the Moei river, serving as a low-key border crossing between the two countries. The flags of Thailand and Myanmar decorate each country's half of the bridge, flapping briskly in the breeze. A short walk to the far end of the bridge will bring you into a different century.

You'll find yourself in Tachileik, a simple village where the women beautify themselves by painting *thanaka* (a yellow paste) on their faces, where the open-air market offers you snack foods you've never imagined, and where you can see young monks at their classes inside the local temple.

The covered, open-air market can be your first stop. Here, an array of small vendors sell everything from flowers to local vegetables to huge trays of golden-hued fried crickets. Many of the sellers squat in front of their wares spread out on the market floor. You might see a girl of ten or a wizened grandmother minding the goods, heads sporting conical woven hats or turban-style cloths. Her brother or husband might offer a collection of CDs along with the vegetables.

 Of course, you can recognize beans, tomatoes, and onions, but what are those long purple things? Sweet potatoes. Look for the fuzzy round rose-colored lychee fruit. You'll find lots of leafy green vegetables, but what are those numerous mounds of dried legumes? The colors range from sandy white to gold to dark chocolate brown.

Ah, here are the giant tubs of rice, all with a different name and a different price flag stuck in the middle.

The "protein" section can be a little daunting, for sure. The fish section displays silvery samples on a long tray, but it's the other things that will get your attention. A woman stands ready with her cleaver to hack off a section of a chicken for you. Piles of sausage-like offerings fill another tray. Numerous sellers offer fried chicken feet. (You'll have no trouble recognizing those.) What exactly lies within the fried dumplings next door? Not exactly sure. Big bowls display fried critters of varying sizes, origin, and numbers of legs, all tumbled together. Grab a handful, if you dare.

Finally, the cooks with their bubbling steel pots and sizzling pans await you. Mohinga soup, a slightly sour fish broth with noodles and vegetables, is boiling away and ready to ladle out. Raw meats on skewers are ready for the chef to toss into the wok, along with spices and a smattering of vegetables for your lunch to go. You might get lucky and find the small, sweet pancakes with an egg or nuts sprinkled on top for a lighter snack.

Be careful with sampling the local foods. Your guide can advise you about anything you'd like to try.

After you've toured the market, a stroll through the back streets of this small town will display simple daily life. A grandmother braids a young girl's hair on a stoop. A woman washes her family's clothes at a common well. Eight young boys cluster around one lucky youngster who has somehow come into possession of a Game Boy. A yellow-robed monk hitches a ride on his friend's motorcycle. A ten-year-old novice carefully chooses which candy he wants most.

As you pass through the streets, you will eventually come to the Buddhist temple of Phra Jow La Keng. The lovely worship hall is spacious and graceful—you'll probably be the only visitor. A school for young monks is attached to the temple, and with a discreet look, you can see them studying under their teacher in their open-air classroom. When the lunch bell rings, all ages will stream out of the classroom and the adjacent dormitory for their midday meal.

And now, hop in a tuk-tuk for an open air, (barely) motorized ride up to Shwedagon Pagoda. Here, the golden spires strike up into the sky, offset by the view over the town and countryside. Outside the temple, a few lonely souvenir vendors ply their trade. Tuk-tuk back down the hill into the village and decision-time: fried crickets or chicken feet?

Alternatively, head back through the dusty streets to the Friendship Bridge to reenter Thailand and your current century. In a perfect world, your guide will now unpack a picnic lunch for you to enjoy in a peaceful setting under some trees before returning to your hotel.

TURKEY

KUŞADASI

EPHESUS PLUS PLUS

The Romans "owned" the Mediterranean Sea for hundreds of years, leaving behind relics of their civilization from Rome to England to Egypt and the eastern Mediterranean shores of Israel and Turkey. You'll find arenas and aqueducts, of course, but also traces of theaters and libraries. One of the best places to tour an ancient Roman city is Ephesus on the shores of Turkey, near the town of Kuşadası.

Founded in the fourth century BCE, it boasts an impressive history, serving as the capital city of Asia Minor. All the big stars from back in the day put their feet up here, including Alexander the Great, Julius Caesar, Mark Antony, and Cleopatra. Eventually St Paul settled in and preached in the arena. See: The Bible.

Its substantial wealth allowed the citizens build one of the Seven Wonders of the Ancient World there, the Temple of Artemis. They also constructed the largest theater in Asia Minor, the Library of Celsus housing 12,000 scrolls, and the second biggest gymnasium of the ancient world. Today, you can walk on the marble streets in the well excavated city center. On either side, you can pop into many state and community buildings, see the interiors of the high-rent district homes, marvel at the two-story facade of the library, and tour the nicely preserved arena.

A lot of people visit Ephesus every year, either as an add-on to Istanbul and Cappadocia or from a cruise ship. The eastern Mediterranean cruise itineraries often depart from Athens or Rome and stop at Kuşadası for this express purpose. A typical tour starts at the top of the hill and brings you down through the town center, ending at the arena.

You can enhance your Ephesus visit by touring the site in the morning and then heading out for some authentic local culture. The nearby town of Şirince (pronounced like syringe) sits atop a hill only five miles east of Selçuk, near the archaeological site. Countless vendors line the main drag, offering you local olive oil, fruits, wines, honey, and other natural products including luscious soaps and *pekmez*, a traditional sweetener made from local fruits. Your streetside shopping will remind you how very Mediterranean the coastline of Turkey really is.

Speaking of wine, town lore holds that the Orthodox Christian Greeks who lived here during the Ottoman Empire won kudos for the excellence of their wine. The Muslim Turks who moved here from Thessaloniki in 1924 restarted winemaking using local fruits including apple, apricot, banana, blackberry, blueberry, mulberry (black and white), mandarin orange, melon, orange, peach, quince, sour (Morello) cherry, and strawberry.

The vendor stalls follow a long, sinuous road through town, allowing ample opportunity for browsing and sampling. The soundtrack includes a call to prayer from the village minaret, as well as donkeys braying, birds chirping, dogs barking, and children playing. It's a town full of life, in the best sense.

If you're working with a good travel advisor, you might find yourself enjoying lunch at a private home nearby, hosted by warm and welcoming locals. A menu of fresh vegetables and fruits, as well as local specialties of Turkish cuisine, will hark back to the regional influences of several thousand years of history. The ambience includes the lovely hilltop breezes and a typical landscape of tall, spiky cypress trees and local flora.

For those on a five-star cruise, the ship's program may offer an optional evening concert in the Roman amphitheater back at Ephesus. If this is an option for you, do it!

If you're overnighting locally, you can arrange a sunset concert for as few as two people. After the site closes for the day, you'll walk through the quiet, ancient streets to the amphitheater. With the sun setting over the golden hills, a chamber orchestra playing, and champagne on offer, you can connect the distant past to the present, pleasing at least three of your senses!

UNITED STATES

C&O CANAL, MARYLAND/VIRGINIA/WASHINGTON, DC
NEW YORK – SOUTHAMPTON, ENGLAND
JFK AIRPORT, NEW YORK
SOUTH CAROLINA
WASHINGTON, DC, MARYLAND AND VIRGINIA

LOCKMASTER HOUSE HOP

The Chesapeake & Ohio Canal (C&O, in local terms) runs 184 miles alongside the Potomac River from Cumberland in western Maryland, past Harpers Ferry, Virginia, eventually ending in Georgetown, Washington, DC. Dug largely by hand in the first half of the 1800s, it suffered many stops and starts before its final completion in 1850. For years, the canal served as a trade route, specifically transporting coal from the Allegheny Mountains. By 1924, however, it was already obsolete.

Along the course of the C&O, its elevation rises as much as six hundred feet. That means locks. Lots and lots of locks raised and lowered boats along the waterway. There are seventy-four of them on the canal and each of them once needed a lockmaster. The lockmaster would manually close the gates, empty or fill the lock as needed, and then open the gates at the end of the process. The lockmasters lived at the lock since boat traffic could arrive at any time. Their small houses remain, although the canal land now serves as a place of recreation, administered by the National Park Service.

In recent years, an interesting development has occurred: some of the lock houses have undergone restoration and furnishing for rental purposes. These small homes suffered abandonment for many years, but the National Park Service has repaired and decorated seven houses, each focusing on a particular era.

These simple structures can house four to eight people in combinations that usually consist of two bedrooms with a trundle bed or two. Most of them are in Montgomery County, Maryland, but Lockhouse 49 is west of Hagerstown. Its décor evokes the 1920s.

Lockhouse 28, dating to 1837, reflects the competition between the canal owners and the B&O railroad owners, each striving to reach the Ohio River Valley first. Eventually the C&O won the right to build next to the river and the railroad got sidelined to a route through the hillside above. You can still notice the active railroad track nearby. The décor of this lock house reflects the 1830s.

Lockhouse 25 near Poolesville, Maryland, began service in 1830 but found itself in the thick of the Civil War. Three separate Confederacy campaigns sought to displace opposing Union forces doing their best to protect the canal. Both sides destroyed locks, dams, and even boats on the canal. Given its history, its decoration reflects the Civil War.

Lockhouse 22 at Pennyfield focuses on mechanics, including construction of aqueducts, lift bridges, incline planes, tunnels, and the all-important locks that allow boat traffic to negotiate the rapids and waterfalls on the river. Notably, Great Falls, twenty-one miles from Washington, presented a BIG problem for navigation. This particular lockhouse reflects the early phase of canal construction because of its lift lock and proximity to Dam Number Two and a guard lock. Décor reflects the 1830s.

Lockhouse 21 was opened in July 2019 and interprets 1916, a time when the canal was changing from a waterway to a recreational area. It focuses on an era when Woodrow Wilson was President, the United States had not yet entered World War I, and the women's movement was beginning.

Lockhouse 10, which sits inside the Beltway, evokes the Depression era of the 1930s. Under FDR, two Civilian Conservation Corps camps provided housing for African American workers who received jobs, education, and training. Along with the workers of the Public Works Administration, these men helped transform the abandoned canal area into the recreational area we see today.

The little stone cottage of Lockhouse 6 sits less than six miles from Georgetown in Washington, DC. After World War II, the Army Corps of Engineers proposed building fourteen dams on the Potomac, which would have overrun the canal and flooded much of the valley. Supreme Court Justice William Douglas had a better idea. In the interest of drawing attention to its hiking possibilities, he challenged the *Washington Post* staff to hike the entire length of the canal with him. In 1954, he took nine editors with him, hiking from Washington, DC to Cumberland, Maryland. After that, the *Post* threw its support behind preservation of the canal as a park, and in 1971, the C&O Canal received that designation.

Lockhouse 6 tells the story of Douglas's commitment to preserving the canal and his challenge to the *Post*. Quite appropriately, its decor reflects the 1950s when he coordinated the hike with the editors.

Imagine a bike trip that traverses the forty miles closest to Washington, DC. Each day you can ride a few miles more, hike along the towpath, and sleep in one of the houses. On your last night, you can stay in Lockhouse 6 and bike six miles into Georgetown for dinner and back to sleep.

Overnight rentals are inexpensive, but reservations are required. Contact the National Park Service to make your arrangements.

TRANSATLANTIC CROSSING

The glamour of the golden age of travel can be yours for seven sweet days on a transatlantic voyage. However, you need to be aware that all transatlantic crossings are not the same because all big ships are not the same.

For example, the major cruise lines all offer "repositioning" cruises when they shift their ships from the Caribbean to Europe for the summer season or back to the Caribbean in the fall. However, a cruise ship designed for the gentle Caribbean waters or to hug the Mediterranean coast is no match for an ocean liner.

For a true transatlantic experience, choose one of the Cunard ships: the Queen Mary 2, the Queen Elizabeth, or the Queen Victoria. These ships can easily handle major bodies of water with their ocean currents and occasional storms. The modern stabilizers on the ocean liners mean that even in gale-force winds, the movement of the ship is minimal. Whether you're a fair-weather sailor, prone to seasickness, or an old salt, you'll be fine. The officers might close the decks if the winds are that strong, but inside the ship, the passengers can carry on with their activities.

About three thousand miles lie between New York and Southampton, England, and the Queen Mary 2 takes seven days to make the journey. She could do it in five because she's fast, but I think the passengers all savor the unique experience of an ocean crossing.

The ocean liners depart from Red Hook in Brooklyn headed to Southampton, UK (or the reverse). When you arrive at the pier, you can only marvel at the leviathan that bobs gently on its moorings. Look up at the gigantic superstructure, with its trademark four black funnels towering above you. You will know innately that this ship is meant for serious things.

Departure from New York occurs with a lot of hoopla and celebration on board and a keen sense of timing. The Cunard ships are enormously tall, so tall that they must time their departure with the tides to fit under the Verazzano-Narrows Bridge. You should head to the top deck to watch the big funnels clear the bridge...just barely.

And out to sea you go, leaving lights, the city, and civilization behind you. As you begin to explore the vast interior of your ship, you'll find numerous dining rooms, bistros, coffee shops, and bars scattered about. If you're a champagne lover, there's a spot for you. If you want to indulge in cigars, there's a special lounge for you. If you like to people watch while sipping a libation, there's a spot for you, too. Search and ye shall find.

The ship offers lots of entertainment in the theater, the planetarium, and the library. You'll be hard pressed to be bored. More important, however, the peace and quiet of the separation from your daily life and the stresses of your normal routines will begin to steal over you as the days pass.

You'll find the topmost deck often sparsely inhabited, even in good weather, and you can walk around on each end of the ship. If you stand on the highest spot and slowly turn 360°, you will see only the vast ocean around you. It's an incredible sight. Perhaps the captain has announced during his noon briefing that the closest spot of land is... the Azores, 1,200 miles to the south!

On a pleasant afternoon, plunk yourself down in a deck chair in the sun. Perhaps you'll read your book. Perhaps you'll gaze out to sea, pondering

your life or many and varied topics. Perhaps you'll chat with your interesting neighbor or your traveling companion. The environment lends itself to activities that we simply don't have time for in our busy lives.

As the ship nears port, get ready for the "Last Night Party" on board. Although an orchestra has played in the main dance hall every other night, with a rock band in the small adjacent nightclub, tonight the rock band takes over the big room. You can feel the festive atmosphere as you enter.

People are happy and smiling; the transatlantic crossing experience has made them that way. As the appointed (and well announced) hour approaches, the staff will hand out small British flags. Suddenly, a burst of patriotic music blares and flags are waved madly. People dance. People sing. A wild party ensues, with great music and fun.

In the morning, your early rising will be rewarded with the sight of land at dawn as the ship nears Southampton. It's magical. You have sailed seven days eastward, and you've really done it. Here is land; here is England to prove it.

THE TWA TERMINAL

Oh, the golden age of transatlantic air travel! Passengers dressed up. No one wore pajamas or basketball shorts. The stewardesses (and they were all "stewardesses") sported stylish and glamorous uniforms. The era of cheap fares, minimal service, and jam-packed skinny seats lay far in the future when TWA hired noted modernist architect Eero Saarinen to design their terminal at JFK.

Saarinen created the Gateway Arch in St. Louis, Dulles Airport outside of Washington, DC, the MIT Chapel in Boston, and the Yale ice hockey rink in New Haven. The TWA terminal at JFK tops them all.

Founded by Howard Hughes, TWA competed directly with Pan Am for the transatlantic air market. By the 1960s, TWA was thriving, and JFK (the renamed Idlewild Airport) was morphing into the behemoth we all know and love today.

Saarinen designed the "winged" terminal to reflect the sensation of flying. Inside, passengers accessed the planes from two long passenger tubes that ascended six feet from ground level. This major innovation meant that passengers didn't get wet while boarding and deplaning during bad weather. Other innovations included

a baggage carousel, closed circuit television, a central PA system, that iconic "electromechanical split-flap display" schedule board, and a cluster of gates away from the main terminal.

TWA began to founder in the 1990s, and by the year 2000, was struggling financially. Twin blows came in the form of the TWA 800 crash and eventually 9/11. In October 2001, American Airlines acquired TWA and its famous terminal.

But American abandoned it and so there it sat, unused but still beloved by many. Happily, in 2019, the TWA Terminal and Hotel reopened as both hotel and public space—and then some. And what will you find there on your visit?

You can enter directly from outside or use one of the passenger tubes now connecting JetBlue to the TWA terminal. The TWA red color dominates everything.

Inside the soaring space of the terminal, you can ask questions from a "pilot" and a "stewardess" at the information desk, when staffed. The electromechanical split-flap display shows imaginary flights to all corners of the world, just like TWA used to offer.

The sunken lounge with its huge windows and Jetsons-style seating serves as a great meeting place and spot for cocktails and conversation. It's all red, red, red.

Upstairs, a balcony hosts a Jean-George Vongerichten restaurant serving simple fare and libations. They offer a tasty hamburger, but at a pretty penny.

In another corner upstairs, check out the display of uniforms for stewardesses and pilots dating to TWA's earliest days. Sadly, it's obvious that the 1970s marked the beginning of the end for flight crew elegance. The Oleg Cassini designs gave way to polyester pantsuits, and it went downhill from there.

After the Sunken Lounge, head for the tarmac and the old Constellation airplane parked outside. Ascend the jetway to enter this storied plane, which served as Air Force One for President Eisenhower. In its current incarnation, a stewardess bartender serves cocktails. You can choose to sit side-by-side in airplane seating or facing inward on plush sofas near the front. Outside the windows, in winter you can gaze down on a small skating rink below.

In warm weather, head to the rooftop for access to the terrace overlooking the active runways of the airport. Guests can dip into a small infinity pool while observing the arriving and departing air traffic. Best of all, friendly bartenders stand nearby to enhance that great ambience.

It's a happy crowd up above. Even on a warm day, the airfield generates breezes, making it a lovely setting for a gentle libation. Watch the planes taxi. Watch them take off. Watch the planes land. Watch the overall ground operation. You and your fellow aviation buffs can snap pictures of the airfield and each other, with an occasional selfie thrown in. You may find yourself chatting with total strangers.

Note: *The TWA hotel uses two new buildings, but only one of them offers runway views. So, make sure you book your room in the right building. Check-in takes place on the main floor of the terminal behind what certainly looks a like an airport check-in counter. Yes, a baggage strip lies behind the desk, although it's not active.*

Whether you choose to stay at the hotel overnight or just drop in for an afternoon, the clerks will hold baggage for you. If you've got a few hours before your flight from a different terminal, you can "check" your bags at the hotel and pick them up when you're ready to hop on the airtrain to your departure terminal.

The iconic Eero Saarinen terminal has risen, phoenix-like, from the ashes of a once-proud airline. You will find it a most welcome addition to one of the world's busiest airports.

Note: *Access to the rooftop terrace carries a fee and requires advance reservations for non-hotel guests.*

GHOST TOUR OF CHARLESTON

Charleston, South Carolina, claims some serious bragging rights in terms of its early American heritage, stately architecture, historic homes, and a well-earned reputation for grace and charm. As you climb into a horse-drawn carriage for a leisurely clip-clop tour of the historic center, you will sense all those elements.

Sadly, you will also encounter the heritage of slavery which comprised a big part of Charleston's early status as a major port city on the east coast. It's hard to reconcile that brutal story with the gracious city we see today, but the truth cannot be ignored. And of course, all American schoolchildren learn that the Civil War began when Southern rebels fired on Fort Sumter in the harbor. Charleston tells many different stories, making it a particularly interesting American city.

You can delve into the local culture even further by participating in an evening ghost tour. Ghost tours often illustrate key things about a town because they retell the stories that people pass down from generation to generation. Since Charleston happens to be one of the most haunted cities in America, a walking tour in the evening adds several layers of depth to the monuments you tour during the day.

Confederacy Vice President John C. Calhoun and his burial site is a "haunting" tale, but the Exchange Building, the old City Jail, and the Dock Street Theatre have great stories, too.

The Old Exchange Building, a historic landmark dating back to 1771, has served many functions over the years, such as a commercial exchange (including the slave trade), customs house, post office, City Hall, military headquarters, and now a museum. Legend says that the infamous pirate Edward Teach (aka Blackbeard) even called it home while imprisoned in the city. Today, the Exchange Building draws major tourist dollars, but the stories of strange goings-on within are legion. Witnesses have reported doors opening and closing on their own, "cold spots," and chains that suddenly start swinging for no apparent reason. Whether or not the alleged moans of pain are real, several very sober citizens have told their personal stories of paranormal phenomena within the building.

The Dock Street Theatre has had a tumultuous past, including fires and even an earthquake, since it opened in 1735. As one of the most haunted places in town, two separate ghosts restlessly roam its halls. One ghost carries the spirit of the famous actor Junius Brutus Booth, the father of Abraham Lincoln's assassin John Wilkes Booth. The second spirit goes nameless but seems to have been a prostitute.

The Unitarian Church Graveyard hosts the ghost of Annabel Lee, the subject of Edgar Allan Poe's famous poem of the same name. Since Annabel's father opposed her seeing Poe, a sailor in the Navy at the time, the two lovers engaged in a forbidden tryst at the cemetery. Even when Annabel Lee died of yellow fever, her father sought to keep the lovers apart. To that end, he dug up all the graves around hers so that the heartbroken Poe wouldn't know at which grave to mourn. Many claim to see Annabel's ghost roaming the cemetery today, still searching for her lost love.

The Mills House Hotel claims to have hosted many famous Americans, including Robert E. Lee and Theodore Roosevelt. Dating back to 1861, the building housed Confederate Soldiers during the Civil War and famously survived a nearby fire. After watching the fire from the roof, General Lee and others returned to the "parlor" and found mothers and babies preparing to exit the building. General Lee took one baby and a fellow officer took the other, bringing them to safety outside the building. Legend holds that the ghosts of the Confederate soldiers haunt the building, asking for water to put out the fire. In addition, staff and guests have seen a spectral woman with a baby in the halls. Notably, when the building was reconstructed in recent times, the number of floors shrank from seven to five. Since the floor levels are not in the same place anymore, this female ghost only appears from the knees up.

Poor John C. Calhoun has never "rested easy" after his death. Initially, the city elders buried him in the western cemetery reserved for "strangers," those unfortunate souls not born within the city limits. However, near the end of the Civil War, the local citizens decided to exhume and rebury him in an unmarked grave in the eastern cemetery to prevent possible desecration by Sherman's army. After the war, the rule about strangers and burial spots resurfaced. Yet again, the citizenry exhumed and returned him to the western cemetery since he was indeed a "stranger." His ghost usually appears clad in a long cape, always looking toward the horizon where his country home lay.

You can tour all these locations, independently. However, the evening guided walking tours share all these great stories and legends. Let's face it: ghost stories are best told face-to-face. Although several companies offer ghost tours in the evening, the Exchange Building is open only during the day. Plan accordingly.

ON THE TRAIL OF JOHN WILKES BOOTH

In a city of monuments to great men (and a few women), Ford's Theatre in Washington, DC, remains a poignant and moving experience for most Americans. After that awful night in 1865 when John Wilkes Booth killed Abraham Lincoln, the theater sat empty for one hundred years. In the 1960s, performances began again in the interior, restored to its appearance in 1865. During the day, you can sit in the seats on the theater floor, looking up at the box in which Lincoln sat and remembering just what we all lost that night. You can also attend a one-hour dramatization in the morning which will add much to your understanding of what happened during that fateful encounter.

A failed actor from a famous acting family, Booth left a trail that still haunts us today. With a little effort and a car, you can track his sorry life immediately before the assassination, his escape from the theater, and his eventual capture and demise in rural Virginia. You'll need a rough idea of the events, but many of the settings and locations are easily identifiable, even today.

First, go to Ford's Theatre and watch the one-hour dramatization, as mentioned above. After the presentation, proceed around the block to the alleyway to see the spot where Booth paid an unsuspecting stagehand to hold his horse ready for his escape. After pulling the trigger, Booth, ever the actor, leapt to the stage shouting, *"Sic semper tyrannis"* (Thus always to tyrants). He broke his leg doing so but managed to mount his horse and ride out of town.

After the theater, walk ten minutes to 541 H Street, NW, now a Chinese restaurant. In 1865, this townhouse served as a boardinghouse run by Mary Surratt. Here, the eight conspirators met repeatedly to plot their revenge on Lincoln. In the aftermath of the assassination, four conspirators hanged, Mary Surratt among them. You'll see a small plaque on the wall, attesting to the building's dark history.

Back in your car, head south to cross the Anacostia River on the Martin Luther King, Jr., Bridge. This bridge is close to the river crossing that Booth and his co-conspirator David Herold used as they fled the city into Maryland.

Heading to Surratt's Tavern, now a museum near modern day Clinton, Maryland, you'll see where the conspirators hid guns, ammunition, and other supplies for use in their original plot to kidnap Lincoln. Mrs. Surratt visited the tavern several times in the days before the assassination, making sure that the supplies were ready for pick up. And in fact, Booth and Herold stopped at Surratt's Tavern as they fled further south, picking up rifles and binoculars.

Next, go to 3725 Dr. Samuel Mudd Road in Waldorf, Maryland. Booth's broken leg needed medical attention, and at 4 am on the morning of April 15th, he and Herold knocked on the door at this house. Dr. Samuel Mudd unwittingly set the anonymous traveler's leg and allowed the fugitives a few hours rest. You can tour the small museum and learn more about the events of that night and how Dr. Mudd paid a heavy price for his actions.

Now, drive south towards Bryantown, Maryland. You will pass through Zekiah Swamp, for which Booth and Herold needed a guide. Eventually you can see the pine thicket near Bel Alton, Maryland, where they camped for five days while Booth wrote a bitter self-defense in his diary. The pine trees are set back along a disused railroad line nears Wills Road.

For the last part of the trail, head further south to Newburg, Maryland. Here, where the river has become much wider, the two men crossed the Potomac one last time to Virginia, in a rowboat.

Near Port Royal, along Route 301, lies the site of Booth's final stop. As they moved about Virginia (a Confederate state), he and Herold posed as Rebel soldiers returning home. But confronted by actual Confederate soldiers, Herold called out, "We are the assassinators of the president!" The real soldiers chose to help them and steered them to the Richard Garrett Farm as a safe haven for sympathizers.

Two weeks after the assassination, Union soldiers had tracked the two men to the farmhouse and the barn. Herold surrendered, but Booth did not. The soldiers set fire to the barn to drive Booth out. However, despite orders, one of the soldiers fired through a gap in the barn siding and hit Booth while he was still inside, severing his spinal cord. He died two hours later.

Today, Route 301 is a four-lane highway with a big grassy median. A small marker along the highway identifies the former site of the farmstead. Some brave souls dare to cross the highway to the median, but you should not attempt to do so. Instead, consider this last location a "drive-by" event.

See the endnotes of this book for publications that can help you plan your day and decide which spots you'd like to visit.

VIETNAM

BEN TRE
DA NANG
HUE

DAYTRIP TO MEKONG DELTA

Saigon (Ho Chi Minh City) visitors often spend two days in that noisy and frenetic city, with one day for a city tour and a second day at Cu Chi to see the Viet Cong tunnels. Consider adding a third day to allow for an excursion out to the peaceful countryside of the Mekong Delta.

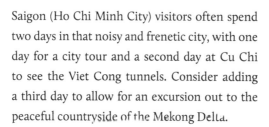

A drive of about ninety minutes can bring you to Ben Tre, a small island where visitors can glimpse traditional Vietnamese life as it has been lived for centuries in this ancient land. History fans will be interested to know that the French colonial forces first conquered the island in the 1860s, but during the Vietnam War, it served as a hotbed of resistance to anti-communist forces led largely by some fierce women soldiers.

Today, Ben Tre is a peaceful small village that does not see nearly the number of tourists as other delta villages. As always, I strongly recommend having a good guide to facilitate your experience.

You might start your visit at the coconut candy "factory." Under a long, low roofed shed, villagers press the coconuts to extract the milk (or juice) from the fruit. The milk is then mixed by hand and cooked in large, steaming woks with "malt" locally made from fermented sticky rice. When it has caramelized sufficiently, the mixture is taken from the wok and laid out on long wooden molds to cool.

In the final step, you'll find a group of women sitting convivially at long tables where they cut and wrap the cooled sweet substance in rice paper while sharing the local gossip about husbands, children, neighbors, and life in general. This is not a factory with industrialized machines, clanging away, but a gentler and more aromatic means of producing a well-known sweet delicacy. And of course, it is for sale right then and there. Warning: a little goes a long way.

And the rice paper? After the coconut candy factory, continue to a local rice paper "factory" under the nearby trees. Here, you can watch women tending the boiling vats of liquid and gently coating what looks like a large paddle with the hot rice paper. You can watch the papermaker gently remove the mixture from the paddle and lay what is now a paper-thin, almost translucent substance on a long rack to cool and dry. Voila! Rice paper.

From here, you can hire a horse and carriage to traverse the rest of the island, but I recommend walking to experience the slow pace of life. You might pass a school with happy children in the school yard. You might watch a man getting his haircut in the barber shop. People walk by, going about their daily business.

Since the village is on an island, add a leisurely sampan float to get you back to the mainland and your transportation back to Saigon.

CLIMBING THE MARBLE MOUNTAINS

A cluster of five small limestone and marble mountains (or very large hills) sits overlooking the coast in central Vietnam, just south of Da Nang. Da Nang served as a major US airbase during the Vietnam War, and the Marble Mountains served as an impregnable hideout for the Viet Cong. In fact, they even used the caves of the mountain as a hospital at one point. Throughout the war, they continually shelled the airbase on numerous occasions from above, lending a military significance to what was traditionally a home for religious shrines.

Today, the mountains are often merely a sight observed from afar as visitors travel between Hue, the old imperial capital, and Da Nang, now the site of a growing number of luxury hotels. Indeed, the coastline is beautiful south of Da Nang, and it is no wonder that hotel construction is a major local enterprise. But with a little effort, visitors can ascend to the top of one of the mountains, Thuy Son. Thuy Son means *water* and the other four mountains are named for earth, metal, fire, and wood.

A drive up to the base of the mountain from the small village below brings you past numerous workshops for stone cutting and stone crafts. Although quarrying directly from the mountains is now banned, the stone cutters' traditional work continues in their shadow.

And so you begin your climb. The stairs are not particularly challenging, and there are numerous spots to "pull over" and catch your breath. And in virtually every nook, you'll find that someone thought it would be perfect for a small pagoda or a shrine to Buddha. Some of them are big; some are small. Some are elaborate; some are quite simple. Some sit on the face of the mountain. Others require you to traverse narrow openings in the rock and access a small chamber. You can count almost 100 shrines on Thuy Son. At times, the local vegetation looks like it's just about to succeed in swallowing up the carvings, but still, they hold their own. Some of the earliest statues date back to the fourteenth and fifteenth centuries!

At 156 steps up, you'll find the 400-year-old Tham Thai Pagoda, probably the best known of the shrines.

As you make your way up, you'll come across a double cave flanked by a side cave with five giant holes at the top, remnants of US bombs dropped from above. Keep looking and you'll see numerous bullet holes, left over from those unhappy days.

Eventually, you'll arrive at Hell Cave, an opening guarded by Hell and Heaven with a giant meditating Buddha within.

Be sure to push on to the very top for a gorgeous view of the city below and the coastline. You can see how easily the mountains control the land below.

The path back down is a lot easier!

Note: *The mountains are not accessible for people with disabilities, and you must be prepared to climb a lot of steps.*

DMZ OF THE VIETNAM WAR

For many Americans, a mention of the Vietnam War conjures up memories of ravaged countryside in a faraway country. Nightly newscasts focused on body counts, firefights near US airbases, and dramatic protests here at home. Happily, the now unified country has moved on from those sad times in many ways and the tourism images now focus on beautiful, misty landscapes, friendly citizens, and ancient and exotic Buddhist Temples. However, if you'd like to pay tribute to the tumultuous time of war, you can easily incorporate a day of remembrance with a visit to the former DMZ (demilitarized zone).

Shortly after the end of World War II, the victorious allies of Britain, France, and the United States watched with alarm as a nationalist movement gained strength in Vietnam. Under the leadership of Ho Chi Minh, the nationalists sought to throw off French rule dating from the middle of the 1800s. Ho Chi Minh had adopted a Communist philosophy by this time, and Vietnam was seen by the Western powers as part of a "domino" chain that could lead to Communist subjugation of Asia. With the assistance of Britain, French rule was reestablished, although in a weakened state.

The growing dominance of the Communists led to a disastrous French battle at Dien Bien Phu, which resulted in the French conceding defeat. Negotiations led to the Geneva Accords of 1954, which divided the country into North and South Vietnam along the 17th Parallel. The line stretched west to east from the border with Laos to the coast. The Viet Cong army dominated North Vietnam, while Ngo Dinh Diem took power in South Vietnam, with support from various Western countries hoping to build a democratic nation.

After the French withdrawal, the US took up the leadership of the fight against Communism and invested heavily in fortifying the border between north and south. The DMZ consisted of a zone five kilometers wide on either side of the Ben Hai River, about two hours north of the imperial capital at Hue. Sadly, the southern section of the DMZ saw some of the fiercest and bloodiest fighting in the war. The battles for Khe Sanh and "Hamburger Hill" took place here with high American casualties.

The Hien Luong Bridge spans the river and illustrates the history of this region by its various incarnations. Originally a wooden pedestrian bridge, the French eventually transformed it into a much more substantial structure. During the war, the two sides constantly raised their flagpoles higher to tower over the opposing flag. Similarly, the bridge was painted over and over in the colors of each side. Today, a cluster of relics speaks to this tortured history.

Khe Sanh was one of the most hard-fought battles of the war, during which a Marine garrison defended their position for seventy-seven days, resulting in heavy casualties on both sides, although considerably more on the North Vietnamese side. Both sides declared victory, for various reasons. Today, you can still see the red-dirt airfield.

To the west lie the Vinh Moc Tunnels, where an entire village lived for two and a half years. Seventeen babies were born in the tunnels. A small but informative museum displays photos of the construction of the tunnels and illustrates daily life underground. If you've already visited the Cu Chi tunnels near Saigon, you might decide to skip the Vinh Moc version.

Actual remnants of the DMZ are few and far between (which is probably a good thing). You may come across a rusted tank and other assorted artifacts. However, a good guide will share the personal stories of the people who lived and died in and around the DMZ during the twenty years of conflict after the Geneva Accords divided the country in two.

Anyone really interested in the Vietnamese version of what is termed "the American War" will get a one-sided picture at the museum in Saigon, which displays various pieces of American war equipment on the grounds.

WALES

SNOWDONIA

LLWYNGWRIL, THE KNITTING TOWN

Wales is full of surprises. Yes, the big modern city of Cardiff, reachable by train from London in about two hours, offers plenty of hotels, restaurants, and museums. However, a good rental car and some leisurely exploration will reward you, the intrepid traveler.

In the northwest corner of Wales is Snowdonia National Park, a mélange of mountains, grassy knolls, lakes, and sheep. And more sheep. Lots of sheep. The park is a hiker's paradise. Even in the warm summer months, it never gets all that crowded, and the landscape is stunning. Come around a corner and watch a huge vista unfold before your eyes.

Small towns are the order of the day, and the hotels are generally of the B&B nature. Ideally, your host will give you directions for a gentle driving tour in the area that includes Llwyngwril, the knitting town. With their town sitting on the edge of the park, the five hundred residents of Llwyngwril knit. They knit big time.

You may be thinking, "Well, what the hell? I knit, too. I made a sweater for my husband and little cap for my nephew and gave them as Christmas presents last year." No, that's not what goes on in Llwyngwril.

Remember all the sheep I mentioned earlier? Lots and lots of sheep make lots and lots of wool. And in the depths of a snowy Welsh winter, beyond the local pub, activity gets a little...well... limited. Perhaps once, a very creative granny went a little stir-crazy and had to be institutionalized—but her kinfolk took inspiration from her. The results speak for themselves.

Even a casual visitor will be struck by knitted creations adorning houses, gates, bridges, cemeteries, taverns, lampposts, benches, and anything else possible. The main road through town will introduce you to the concept, but turn down any street and you'll discover more—and more—and more.

You can see a life-size portrayal of a witch, well-appointed with scarves and a hat, accompanied by a spider. Understand that the entire creation is knitted, not just the accessories.

You might find teddy bears on the cemetery gate. A fetching young lass in a scarlet dress with attractive leggings and decorative neckwear decorates a house. You might favor the very large and friendly dog on a fence. Or the charming tableau of a playground picnic with sheep on a seesaw and first-prize doggie. Or the dog on a dirt bike. Or a multicolored bicycle. Or a tree of fish. Or a Scottish woman of a certain age in local garb. The troll coming up over the side of the bridge as you come through town represents a local legend of the town. Sadly, he has been stolen, recreated, and stolen again. But the knitters keep knitting, undeterred.

The correct term for this art form is yarn bombing or urban knitting. And of course, the creations are perishable, especially if you consider what the weather is like in England and Scotland and Wales. In case you didn't know, they get a lot of rain there. Thus, visitors in successive years will probably see very different renditions.

Perhaps the unusual creativity of Llwyngwril will spur you to make an annual pilgrimage just to see what's new.

Note: *Despite the colorful theories I expressed above, the knitting frenzy actually began in 2015 as a project to raise money for a local community center. Two enterprising women invited residents to join them, and the project took off from there. It's been very successful and, happily, it shows no sign of stopping!*

THE MACH LOOP

Channel your inner Tom Cruise and prepare to hone your dogfighting talents. Ok, admittedly, few of us will ever complete the US Navy "Top Gun" training course and fly an F-15. However, you can certainly watch American and British fighter pilots practice their skills VERY, VERY close to you at the Mach Loop in Wales.

On the edge of Snowdonia Park, between the towns of Dolgellau and Machynlleth, a series of valleys serves as a low-altitude training ground for fighter jets from both the Royal Air Force and the US military. From certain vantage points, you can actually see them flash by BELOW you.

What does a "low-altitude training ground" consist of? The British military operates Tactical Training Areas (TTA) for use in low flying training by fast jets and Hercules transport aircraft. An air force considers low altitude flying an essential skill for fighter pilots and the training replicates what he or she would encounter in a combat situation. Generally, the pilots fly at altitudes between 100 and 250 feet, when weather conditions allow.

When a training area is active, routine low flying by other military users can take place between 500 feet and 2,000 feet. Although the pilots train Monday through Friday throughout the year, late spring and summer are the busiest times for low flying since the squadrons make full use of good weather.

An interested observer might see Royal Air Force Airbus A400Ms, Typhoons, Hawk jets and C-130J and Short Tucanos, as well as US Air Force F-15C Eagles and F-15E Strike Eagles. The F-15s are based at RAF Lakenheath, and MC-130s and V-22 Ospreys operate from RAF Mildenhall. Occasionally, aircraft from other European nations have been sighted training in the Mach Loop too, such as Belgian F-16 Stingers.

So, how do you get to see the fighter jets in action? Like the Northern Lights, a sighting cannot be guaranteed. However, you can certainly combine a number of variables for a very good chance of seeing them screaming past, very, very low over the lush green hillsides of these rural valleys.

Plan to make a three-day visit to Wales in late spring or summer. That should give you enough time to get a sunny day without wind during the week, the optimal timeframe for the training site to be active.

The UK government publishes a short-range timetable of training "slots," which you can find online. You'll see that the site shows the planned schedule for about three weeks in advance. Pay attention to the word *planned* since weather conditions determine everything. You'll see that in the schedule, the flight windows are well defined during the day.

Enthusiasts can also consult spotterguide.net Here, you can find detailed instructions on how to access the five best viewing spots: Bluebell, Corris Corner, Upper Bwlch, Lower Bwlch, CAD East, and CAD West.

You will definitely need a car, since no public transportation can take you to the viewing areas. In some cases, you'll find small parking lots. In other places, you will need to leave your car on the shoulder of the road.

You will also need sturdy walking shoes. Some areas offer paths; others will require traversing open land. You will need to walk up, up, up.

Unsurprisingly, this activity does not accommodate people with mobility issues.

The hilltops are windy. Be prepared to bring a portable chair or blanket to sit on. In particular, if you are planning to use a vantage point with a formal parking area, you will need to come early to secure a spot. Furthermore, you will not find facilities for restroom breaks or food, so build those considerations into your planning.

These hills are private land. The landowners do allow aviation buffs to traverse their property, but they're not required to do so. Be considerate as you visit and respect the countryside, leaving no trace of your visit behind as you depart.

You will probably be able to see the pilots in their cockpits as they streak by. You might be inspired to wave, but just be aware that they're pretty busy keeping their eyes focused on the task at hand.

If you're willing to travel to Wales, rent a car, put on your hiking shoes, climb a hill, and settle in for a few hours on a windy hilltop, you will experience a unique thrill as these planes roar by you. You should get some great pictures!

John Wilkes Booth Assassination Trail: For history buffs tracking John Wilkes Booth's final days, the following sources will be useful:

"How to Follow John Wilkes Booth's Escape Route: A self-guided tour," by Eddie Dean, *The Washingtonian*, April 10, 2015. https://www.washingtonian.com/2015/04/10/how-to-follow-lincoln-assassin-john-wilkes-booths-escape-route/

"Retracing John Wilkes Booth's escape route," by David Montgomery, *The Washington Post*, April 14, 2015. https://www.washingtonpost.com/news/arts-and-entertainment/wp/2015/04/14/retracing-john-wilkes-booths-escape-route/

"Manhunt: Tracing the Escape Route of John Wilkes Booth," by Malcolm Logan, in Discovering America One Town at a Time, Aug. 24, 2010. http://myamericanodyssey.com/manhunt-tracing-the-escape-route-of-john-wilkes-booth/

"Tracking an Assassin," by Sarah Mark, *The Washington Post*, April 14, 1995. https://www.washingtonpost.com/wp-srv/local/longterm/tours/civilwar/booth.htm

"Escape DC: The John Wilkes Booth Way," by Marianne Kyriakos, *The Washington Post*, Sept. 26, 1986. https://www.washingtonpost.com/archive/lifestyle/1986/09/26/escape-dc-the-john-wilkes-booth-way/880475aa-dcb1-4b0e-9436-22c79adbf47c/

"Following the Trail of John Wilkes Booth," by Elizabeth C. Mooney, *The Washington Post*, Nov. 30, 1983. https://www.washingtonpost.com/archive/lifestyle/travel/1983/11/20/following-the-trail-of-john-wilkes-booth/54c41547-7283-4ccb-b80d-1dc98d67952c/

Cover: Photo copyright © Ubonwan Utachkul | Dreamstime.com

Pg 9: Photo courtesy and copyright © Tourism Australia

Pg 19: Photo copyright © Sorin Colac | Dreamstime.com

Pg 27: Photo copyright © Lakhesis | Dreamstime.com

Pg 31: Photo copyright © Curtis Smith | Dreamstime.com

Pg 41: Photo copyright © Emicristea | Dreamstime.com

Pg 47: Photo copyright © Ignasi Such | Dreamstime.com

Pg 51: Photo copyright © Evgeniya Moroz | Dreamstime.com

Pg 55: Photo copyright © Donyanedomam | Dreamstime.com

Pg 61: Photo copyright © Padchas | Dreamstime.com

Pg 69: Photo copyright © Elena Elisseeva | Dreamstime.com

Pg 79: Photo copyright © Rudi1976 | Dreamstime.com

Pg 87: Photo copyright © Saletomic | Dreamstime.com

Pg 91: Photo copyright © Stefano Valeri | Dreamstime.com

Pg 101: Photo copyright © Cezary Wojtkowski | Dreamstime.com

Pg 119: Photo copyright © Raul Garcia Herrera | Dreamstime.com

Pg 127: Photo copyright © Iñigo Arza Azcorra | Dreamstime.com

Pg 131: Photo copyright © William Perry | Dreamstime.com

Pg 135: Photo copyright © Dudlajzov | Dreamstime.com

Pg 141: Photo copyright © Padchas | Dreamstime.com

Pg 149: Photo copyright © Lian Deng | Dreamstime.com

Pg 155: Photo copyright © Kasto80 | Dreamstime.com

Pg 159: Photo copyright © Kierran Allen | Dreamstime.com

Pg 163: Photo courtesy and copyright © Tourist Office of Spain in New York (TURESPAÑA)

Pg 173: Photo copyright © Sean Pavone | Dreamstime.com

Pg 177: Photo copyright © Llopartic | Dreamstime.com

Pg 179: Photo copyright © Ihorga | Dreamstime.com

Pg 183: Photo courtesy and copyright © Zermatt-Matterhorn

Pg 189: Photo courtesy and copyright © Anantara Golden Triangle Elephant Camp & Resort

Pg 197: Photo copyright © Ryhor Bruyeu | Dreamstime.com

Pg 201: Photo copyright © Sean Pavone | Dreamstime.com

Pg 213: PPhoto copyright © Nikosleontis | Dreamstime.com

Pg 221: Photo copyright © Gail Johnson | Dreamstime.com

Diana Hechler, President of D. Tours Travel in Larchmont, NY, traces her passion for travel to a childhood in Italy and a father with an "itchy foot". As a college student, she spent a magical summer backpacking around Europe with a friend and dreamed of running her own travel company one day. In 1999, she opened the doors at D. Tours Travel and started happily planning and producing authentic adventures around the world for her clients.

Ms. Hechler holds a Master's Degree in Law & Diplomacy from the Fletcher School at Tufts University and a B.A. from Middlebury College. In addition to earning various destination credentials, she has been named to the Top 25 Travel Agents list by Travel Agent Magazine.

D. Tours Travel
914.833.9411
www.dtourstravel.com

Printed in the USA
CPSIA information can be obtained
at www.ICGtesting.com
LVHW072229080923
757545LV00062B/1703